GARDENALIA

Sally Coulthard

GARDENALIA
Creating the Stylish Garden

RIZZOLI
NEW YORK

New York · Paris · London · Milan

First published in the United States of America in 2012 by
Rizzoli International Publications, Inc.
300 Park Avenue South
New York, NY 10010
www.rizzoliusa.com

Originally published in the United Kingdom in 2012 by
Jacqui Small LLP
an imprint of Aurum Press Ltd
7 Greenland Street
London NW1 0ND

Publisher Jacqui Small
Managing Editor Kerenza Swift
Editor Sian Parkhouse
Designer Laura Woussen
Picture Researcher Claire Hamilton
Production Peter Colley

2012 2013 2014 2015 / 10 9 8 7 6 5 4 3 2 1

ISBN: 978-0-8478-3877-6
Library of Congress Control Number: 2012933833

Printed in China

PAGE 1 *From formal stone urns to vintage laundry tubs, rustic wooden benches to well-worn wicker baskets, a picture perfect selection of well-loved gardenalia.* PAGE 2 *In the season of mists and mellow fruitfulness, fall's perennial chores feel infinitely more pleasurable with the help of rustic tools, weathered watering cans, and robust woven containers.* RIGHT *The perfect potting shed. Thrift-shop bargains, timeless tools, and handcrafted objects work together to bring a practical but prettily decorative flourish.*

Contents

INTRODUCTION

There's more to gardening than plants. From decoration to cultivation, we rely on all sorts of tools, containers, furniture, and ornaments to turn garden dreams into reality.

Instead of buying new, many of us are using vintage gardenalia to breathe new life into our gardens. Whether it's a city balcony or period kitchen garden you own, garden antiques, flea-market finds, and objets trouvés are being used in rich and imaginative ways.

All kinds of gardenalia can create timeless yet exciting spaces: gates, fences, and follies—the bones of a garden; spades, sifters, pots, and trowels—the tools we need to do the hard work; seating and lighting—to help us relax and entertain; and finishing touches—statues, urns, water fountains, and figurines.

Nothing can match the patina of an antique lead planter or handmade basket. Stacks of terra-cotta pots, rows of vintage tools, a pretty shed with flaking paint are all visual treats that add to the overall impact of a garden. Nothing is too old, too shabby, or too worn—weathering and repeated use only seem to enhance the appeal of a piece of gardenalia, rather than diminish it.

And, as we fill our terra-cotta pots with earth or dig away with an old wooden trowel, we're reconnecting with our memories. In the hustle and bustle of modern life, we're keen to surround ourselves with things from a simpler, slower time. It's pure nostalgia, but we're better for it.

In a flat-pack world, gardenalia helps us be different. You can create your own, totally unique garden. Whether it's a piece of driftwood or a decorative statue, no two pieces are ever the same. Thanks to gardenalia, you can create formality, play with perspective, inject warmth, or, best of all, add a bit of fun to your flower beds.

RIGHT In this cozy corner of a relaxed, walled garden, classic elements of gardenalia—the decorative wirework chair, park bench, zinc tools, and glass cloche—combine to create a simple but elegant display of garden bygones.

Sourcing

The treasure hunt for gardenalia is part of its charm and the more obscure the source, the better your chance of bagging a bargain. Salvage yards are a great place to start. They vary in their setup; some are only one step up from a garbage dump, while others are more akin to a well-organized museum. Most reclamation yards tend to be on the scruffier end of the scale, but that's part of their appeal; there's more potential for a discovery, and rooting around among stacks of crusty artifacts satisfies the archaeologist in everyone. Leave your shopping list at home and go with an open mind. Salvage yards never have the same stock two days running. If you see something that grabs you, buy it.

OPPOSITE AND ABOVE **All the fun of a treasure hunt. Shopping for garden salvage always uncovers excellent surprises. From a stately three-tiered fountain to an ornate cast-iron panel and a colonial plant stand, there's no limit to the breadth of bargains for a keen-eyed reclamation rummager.**

Specialist gardenalia dealers are a different proposition. Their knowledge and expertise are invaluable if you are looking for something specific or an investment piece. Treat it like going to an antiques dealer. Go with ideas and a budget in mind. If you can't see what you are looking for on the day, give the dealer a chance to source the item for you. Stone, lead, and ironwork of any weight or value needs to transported and installed with care—make sure that the dealer arranges this for you and that this process is insured.

Auctions can be a rich source of garden antiques. Larger auction houses hold regular sales of high-end garden statuary and collectibles. If you can't attend in person you can often bid online—just remember to factor in delivery and handling costs. Some of the larger pieces, especially stoneware, can be as expensive to ship as they are to purchase, so get quotes for delivery before you commit to buy. Consider farm sales, too. It's not that long ago that many pieces of

gardenalia sold cheaply. Staddle stones, troughs, millstones, and apple presses would pass through farm sales in their thousands and barely raise an eyebrow. Nowadays, these and similar pieces are snapped up at high prices. It's frustrating, but reflects the rising popularity of our agricultural heritage. For the inventive gardenalia user, however, there are pieces that don't come with such a steep price tag—buckets, feeders, tools, and plowing implements are still affordable, especially if they've come to the end of their useful farming life.

ABOVE AND OPPOSITE **Gardenalia can span the centuries. From classic antique to modern retro, there's something to suit all styles of garden, including flamboyant nineteenth-century** *iron furniture, humble turn-of-the-century terra-cotta seedling pots, and lollipop-kitsch 1950s and 1960s chairs.*

Structure and Furnishings

Boundaries

Good fences make good neighbors. But there's more to garden boundaries than marking out your territory. Boundaries are intriguing places—they are the lines that separate public spaces from private, wild from cultivated land, and formal areas from informal—so why not be creative with their design?

From whimsical driftwood to ornate iron panels, reclaimed materials and quirky gardenalia will delineate your plot but also create focal points and hidden corners, provide visual definition, and offer protection for plants.

Fences

Gardeners have always been a fussy bunch. We demand that anything we use in the garden has to be functional. But, as aesthetes, we also like it to be beautiful. And with good reason. We pour our hearts and souls into the planting side—choosing plant colors and varieties with great aplomb—so it seems a shame to spoil the look with off-the-shelf, pressure-treated fence panels.

Thanks to gardenalia, the alternatives are numerous, especially if you want a warm, organic look. From post-and-rail to woven willow, fences lend themselves naturally to reclaimed wood and found timber. It's a forgiving, characterful material, and can improve with age. Old weathered wood comes in a myriad of colors—from rich dark browns to silvery grays—and will often have all the bumps, grooves, and knocks that can bring a fence to life. Layers of peeling paint, previous wood stains, or lettering only add to the patina and effect, so don't be tempted to over-restore your salvaged wood if you're after the weather-beaten, distressed look.

Salvaged floorboards, scaffolding planks, driftwood, barn timbers, old sheds, old doors and cupboards, wooden signs, broom handles, headboards, window frames, secondhand stock fencing—there's a wide variety of material and forms at your disposal. You'll be reusing a valuable resource too—garden timber isn't always sourced responsibly, so you'll be recycling an increasingly costly material and reducing the pressure on existing lumber forests.

PREVIOUS PAGES *Sheltering under the wisteria, this intimate seating area was created from the simplest of materials. Wooden trellis and uprights create the walls of a garden room, including a whimsical window to add humor. Café chairs and a vintage table complete the reassuringly romantic look.* LEFT *Beach and lakeside driftwood can* *be cleverly repurposed into informal wooden fencing. The natural silver color, caused by bleaching from the sun, creates a gentle visual backdrop for planting.* OPPOSITE *Partly practical, partly playful, these reclaimed planks and poles create a relaxed boundary in the garden. Vintage pots act as cheerful cane toppers and echo the forms of the flowers.*

When you are using reclaimed timber or found wood, there are some practical considerations to think about. Untreated wood will naturally rot when left outside. If you're not worried about replacing your fence after a few years, leave it to simply decay gracefully and enjoy the process. Not all gardeners want permanence—there's beauty in the idea that any physical boundaries are as fleeting and ever-changing as your plants. Enthusiastic climbers such as honeysuckle, roses, clematis, and ivy will enhance this rambling, faded-glory effect and soon become part of the boundary structure.

If you're keen to have the character, but want it to last, it's worth knowing that certain woods are more resistant to decay than others. Oak, cedar, Douglas fir, pitch pine, and redwood all cope well outside, even untreated. Willow and hazel hurdles can last up to ten years, depending on how exposed your garden is, while other woods—pine, ash, and beech—are less hardy and will need some form of eco-friendly stain, paint, or preservative. Treat the whole

fence, but pay special attention to anywhere where the timber meets the ground, such as the bottom of fence posts.

As with any changes to a boundary, if you're going to build or alter a fence, it's common courtesy to talk to your neighbor about it first. You'll need to establish that you own the fence, and custom dictates that any fence posts are entirely on your land and the "face" of the fence, if there is one, points toward your neighbors.

OPPOSITE *Scaffolding planks and reclaimed floorboards create instant vertical height and effective screening. Salvaged wood is not only eco-friendly and durable but it's also packed with patina, character, and the inherent charm of the imperfect.*

ABOVE *The perennial task of pruning and coppicing trees often leaves behind a rich source of free timber. Straight sections of unwanted branches were used here in a delicately formal way to create neatly geometric but naturalized fencing.*

Metal railings

Metal fencing was always the preserve of people with means. Estate fencing, tree guards, and metal railings were all expensive to manufacture and reserved for the homes of the well-to-do. Prior to the Industrial Revolution, metal fencing would have been made from wrought iron, fashioned by the local blacksmith for prestigious clients. By the nineteenth century, however, improvements in cast-iron technology brought metal fencing within reach of the larger, ever-growing population—domestic architecture, public buildings, and parks were festooned with poker-straight railings, ornate iron panels, finials, and fancy fencing.

Both wrought- and cast-iron fences regularly find their way into salvage yards, reclaimed from demolition sites and house renovations. Both types of fencing transfer seamlessly to the modern garden setting, adding elegance, drama, and structural impact to any space. Single ornate pieces can create show-stopping focal points or act as elaborate plant supports, while larger stretches of fencing make a fine job of delineating formal areas or breaking up large spaces into smaller "rooms." Estate fencing always looks fantastic on either side of a long driveway, while sections of rowhouse railings can make ideal trellising and screening, adding instant height to the back of borders.

Reclaimed ironwork isn't cheap, however, and its condition is key. Rust isn't necessarily a problem, and for many people part of the aesthetic appeal, but you need to make sure that it hasn't taken deep hold, especially on joints and corners. Layers of paints can be easily removed, but cast iron is more brittle and difficult to repair than wrought iron, so check for cracks, breakages, and missing sections before you buy, especially on larger pieces.

LEFT *A delightful stretch of lavish iron fencing creates a strong visual horizontal line in this formal garden. Its sumptuous curves and leaflike patterns help to blend the topiary and simple planting with this confident boundary.*
OPPOSITE *Wrought-iron fencing is used here not only to create a delicate boundary but also as a robust plant support. The curved top sections of these reclaimed panels form floral "swags" onto which clumps of rose-laden climbers can cling, striking a romantic note.*

Walls

Our gardens have become the places we retreat to at the end of a busy day. With so many of us crammed into increasingly smaller plots, however, creating a substantial but appealing garden boundary is top of our priority. Building a solid wall, whether it's from reclaimed bricks or natural stone, not only satisfies our need for privacy and security, but also has the added benefits of reducing outside ambient noise and providing an excellent climbing surface for plants. The soft, rich tones of a handmade brick wall also make the ideal backdrop for sculpture, benches, and other focal points—a sympathetic canvas in front of which you can place more colorful or ornate gardenalia.

Both reclaimed brick and stone are ideal for use in the gardens of older properties, especially if you take care to match and blend your materials with the vernacular style of your house. Experimenting with different bonds can also add pattern and form to your boundary wall. Handmade bricks and natural stone will never fade or bleach; they only get better as they age. The charm of a weathered, lichen-covered wall adds mellowness and maturity to a garden, even if the layout and planting are entirely new.

Half-height and dwarf walls, created from logs, reclaimed bricks, and other substantial materials, can be clever devices for drawing the eye around a flat plane. Curved or winding walls invite the eye to follow their snaking trail, taking our interest from one section of the garden to another. Straight, low walls, in contrast, bring instant formality and order to lawned or planted areas.

ABOVE RIGHT *Reminiscent of a farmer's drystone wall, this knee-height garden boundary lends a mellow, rural feel to a wildflower garden. Lichen and moss add to the sense of maturity and timelessness of this space.* RIGHT *Curving walls draw our eye around the garden but can be expensive to create. An ingenious use of sawn logs creates an instant and economical alternative to brick or stone while also providing a haven for colonizing plants and insect life.* OPPOSITE *This reclaimed brick wall provides a subtle, weathered backdrop for a potted selection of gardenalia; its muted brickwork tones of creams, pinks, and browns provide a pleasing echo in the bench, pots, and plants. The heat that bricks naturally trap will create a warm resting spot on a sunny day.*

LEFT *Gates form an important part in the architecture of a garden. Here, gothic-style post tops and uprights mimic the historic building behind, drawing our eye from the gateway across the lawn and toward the house.*

Gates

Apart from their obvious practical purpose, gates are a simple way to bring decoration into any garden and a valuable tool for adding intrigue and surprise. Nothing is more enticing than a garden gate, slightly ajar. It beckons us to come closer, to explore the space beyond. Everyone loves the idea of a gateway and what lies behind—it's the timeless, childhood notion of the secret garden.

Vintage and antique gates add greatly to this fairy-tale effect. From the stately glamour of wrought iron to the cottage charm of silvered wood, there is a style and shape to suit all gardens and budgets. The sunny, optimistic designs of the 1950s lend a lighthearted retro feel, while nineteenth-century estate gates are undeniably crisp and formal. Whichever type you choose, each gate has its own personality and potential to influence the mood

of your garden. Solid wooden gates, especially if they are head-height or taller, deliberately mask what's beyond, adding intrigue and a sense of security. Gates that allow you to see through them reveal glimpses of vistas, enticing visitors to investigate further and funneling movement through a space.

On a practical level, secondhand and collectible gates are as easy to build into a garden design as their modern counterparts. The only note of caution is to check all the working parts, locks, and pin-hinges—the gate needs to be able to hold itself safely off the ground and cope with regular movement. Broken or unrestorable gates don't necessarily have to be consigned to the scrap heap, however—ornate examples can be reemployed as screens, trellising, wall art, or glass-covered tabletops.

Style choices

- Take clues from the house, echoing any distinctive shapes or vernacular quirks.
- Tall gates look elegant between high hedges or in a walled garden.
- Low gates are practical and pretty in cottage gardens and potagers.
- Freeform gates can be woven from old wood and flexible willow.
- Gates with bars frame a view, pulling your focus forward.

Surfaces

Lawn isn't always the best surface for outdoor surfaces. In many outside spaces you need something harder and more durable than grass, or a material that can cope with heavy shade or full sun. Reclaimed materials, with their inherent strength and age-worn appearance, are the ideal starting point when you're thinking about garden surfaces and paths. From hand-thrown bricks to home-made mosaics, salvaged planks to glass bottle edging, with gardenalia you can create winding paths, relaxing terraces, and so much more.

Brick

Gardeners have used brick flooring for hundreds of years. As a material, it makes perfect sense. It is hard wearing, weather resistant, and tends not to be as slippery as other types of hard surfaces. Size is also fundamentally important to its success—small units are much easier to lay in restricted spaces and are forgiving of undulating surfaces. Few gardens are truly level—bricks can absorb the gentle rolls and slumps without looking uneven or creating tripping hazards. You can also create intricate patterns with brickwork—from herringbone and basket-weave designs to free-flowing shapes and lines.

Reclaimed bricks are in high demand, not least because they provide an instant period charm and handcrafted appeal. Each brick is slightly different both in form and color, creating a soft, patchwork effect when used in large numbers. Bricks are also the ultimate vernacular building material—there are striking regional differences in color and shape due to the different compositions of local clay and historical techniques of each manufacturer.

Using reclaimed bricks for outdoor ground-level surfaces does come with a note of caution. Not all bricks were created equal. Some types of handmade bricks were designed to be used only for inner walls of buildings, where frost-resistance wasn't a priority, while others were hardy enough to be used on the external walls. The two sometimes get mixed together in the reclamation process, but a reputable salvage dealer should be able to tell you whether the bricks are suitable for the job. Better still, used reclaimed brick pavers that were deliberately designed to be used at floor level and are eminently resistant to frost.

LEFT *Reclaimed bricks laid in a herringbone or opus spicatum pattern bring depth and detail to this garden path. Its precise mathematical layout creates a decorative and engaging contrast with cheerfully unruly plants.*

OPPOSITE *Perfection can look out of place in a garden. Here, large reclaimed brick pavers create a handmade path with reassuringly wobbly edges that soften the area of hard-standing and draw the eye to an enticing, sunny seating area.*

OPPOSITE **No two antique stone setts are the same. This uniqueness—which was created when each stone block was cut by hand—produces modern-day paths that are bursting with character and personality.** RIGHT **Offcuts were used to create a stepping stone path, perfect for a cottage garden. Surrounded by a sea of gravel, these smaller sections of stone are not only easier to lay but also cheaper to buy than larger, more pristine flagstones.** FAR RIGHT **Smooth pebbles interspersed with terra-cotta pavers form a gently naturalized path, perfect for a beachside garden or relaxed kitchen garden.**

Stone

From limestone to slate, sandstone to marble, stone makes a graceful and entirely practical choice for garden surfaces. It's also spectacularly heavy, so historically most houses used stone gathered from nearby quarries and transported only a few miles. Nowadays, much of our building stone comes from India and China, but there are compelling ecological and aesthetic reasons for reusing reclaimed stone around your garden.

Stone is expensive to quarry and to move, both in terms of energy and human effort. To reuse such a valuable resource makes sound environmental sense. Weathered and foot-worn stone is also deeply beautiful—it's a look impossible to re-create overnight. Adding reclaimed stone to a garden makes the space feel timeless, adding immediate mellowness and sophistication.

There are a number of ways stone can be used effectively as landscaping. Large stone flags, while expensive, cover a large area quickly, providing a stable, even finish. These are ideal for entertaining areas, such as patios, where tables and their surrounding chairs need a reliably flat surface.

Salvaged stone pavers, which are small square chunks of stone, can be used to create exciting patterns and shapes and, because they were cut by hand in quarries, have a pleasing variation in color, size, and texture. Pavers are also sometimes called setts, cubes, or cassies.

Cobbles, which are essentially large pebbles, make excellent garden paths, but as with all stone the finish depends on the skills of the person laying the material. If you spend the money on the material, leave enough in the budget for a professional landscaper.

Wood

The past decade has seen a boom in people using decking in their gardens. Most people head straight for their local hardware store for cheap lumber, but reclaimed lumber offers a rich source of characterful and inexpensive flooring for your outside space.

As with many forms of gardenalia, there is a compelling green argument for using reclaimed wood. Huge quantities of perfectly sound wood are sent to landfills every year. Much of it comes from the demolition of older properties, where the lumber used is often high-quality pitch pine, redwood, oak, and elm—all species in high demand today. With a little effort—such as removing old nails, replaning, or sanding—this old-growth lumber provides a rich, durable construction material, retaining all the patina and distress marks that give wood real personality.

Whether you want to create a walkway or a veranda, a patio or a plinth, it's important to treat any lumber that you use outside. Water is the enemy of wood, so it's vital that you raise any lumber off the ground to prevent water saturation, as well as giving your planks a good lashing of eco-friendly preservative or paint. Conventional lumber treatments can be toxic to wildlife, soil, and plants, so check before you buy. Using naturally durable wood will also reduce the need for preservatives—American oak, sweet chestnut, western red cedar, larch, and Douglas fir are all good choices.

OPPOSITE *The owners of this garden used reclaimed lumber to create a clever boardwalk that winds through the space. The marshlike planting and raised platform magically disguise the fact that this is an urban garden.* RIGHT *Walkways add an exciting element to the garden, allowing the visitor to "float" above the planting. Reclaimed lumber was used simply but effectively here, providing a sturdy but sympathetic material that blends seamlessly with the surrounding greenery.*

Found materials

While reclaimed brick and stone can be costly, there are plenty of low-budget alternatives for the resourceful and imaginative gardener. From sherds of broken china and terra-cotta to old porcelain tiles and shells, the garden is a fantastic place to show off your treasure-hunted finds and objets trouvés. Salvaged concrete slabs, fossils, beach-combed glass pebbles, and glass bottles laid bottom up—lots of junkyard finds and salvaged goodies translate into landscaping.

There are a few basics to stick to. Any material for use outside has to be able to withstand the elements. The repeated effects of sun, wind, rain, and frost will wreck many objects so it's important to stick to materials that either occur naturally outside—such as shells or pebbles—or have been created to be waterproof or weather-resistant—such as terra-cotta, brick, and glass. Safety is also paramount. Certain highly polished or mirrored surfaces will become perilous if wet, while little feet will need protecting from sharp edges

and rough surfaces. A good solution is to set items into cement or lime-based mortar, creating a visually interesting but essentially flat surface. Mosaics are traditionally created this way, but you can create quirky sections of flooring by using marbles, saucers, cutlery, buttons, small pieces of mirror, or old coins. If it all sounds a bit odd, don't worry, you're in good company. From Victorian grotto floors made from animal bones and teeth to the ultrahip peach pit floors in today's high-end design magazines, it seems we've always been creative with our found materials.

To soften the edges of any area of hard standing, consider leaving pockets of gravel and soil between materials to encourage grass, wildflowers, or herbs to flourish. Certain plants withstand being constantly trampled—plants with a high foot-traffic tolerance include brass buttons (*Leptinella squalida*), creeping varieties of thyme, blue star creeper, and chamomile.

OPPOSITE *Found surfaces can be as abstract and colorful as the planting they complement. Mosaics bring intense splashes of color to this garden. There is a pleasing lack of symmetry and tidiness that ties in skillfully with the eclectic flowers and foliage.* ABOVE LEFT *Terracotta heraldic tiles, beautifully weathered and overgrown, create the feel of a rediscovered medieval path.* ABOVE RIGHT *Upturned wine bottles set into the ground make a sparkling visual display and a robust nonslip surface from a material that might otherwise end up in a landfill.*

LEFT *Crazy paving potsherd style. Terra-cotta pots soon get broken in frosty conditions, but this resourceful gardener has turned garbage into recycled flooring by arranging loose pieces into a cohesive pattern.*

Edging

Garden edging is an integral part of any design and a place where gardenalia can really come into its own. Edges do a number of important tasks: they create boundaries and visual definition, help to break up the monotony of large spaces, add a change of pace, and, most importantly, provide physical barriers between different surfaces.

Railroad ties are often used as a quick and robust form of edging, especially for raised beds where their strength and durability can cope with large volumes of soil. In the past, many ties were treated with creosote as a preservative, but the use of reclaimed railroad ties treated with creosote in playgrounds or in gardens where there may be a risk of frequent skin contact or food contamination is no longer recommended. That shouldn't be a problem if you are using creosote-treated ties for path or lawn edging, but if you want to build raised beds for vegetables, stick to salt-treated or untreated ties.

Beyond the industrial chic of railroad ties, there are lots of smaller reclaimed materials that make excellent edging and add whimsy and humor. Terra-cotta roof tiles, timber logs, old glass bottles, clay drainage pipes, reclaimed slate, Victorian rope-edge, Gothic edging tiles, cast-iron wheels, rocks, clam shells, vintage plates, driftwood, metal hoops, old tools, handmade bricks, rope, dwarf-height iron railings, and even hubcaps, boots, and bowling balls have been employed by ingenious gardeners.

ABOVE LEFT *Cross sections of timber logs make an inexpensive and subtle choice for edging. Laid in a row, these small circles caterpillar along the edge of the lawn, helping to create a practical and visual boundary between grass and planting.* LEFT *Rope-edge or barley twist tiles were a favorite among Victorian gardeners and have now become collectible. Some of the more popular designs are available as reproductions, but nothing matches the period charm of the original glazed terra-cotta versions even if they display some signs of wear and tear.* OPPOSITE *Railroad ties create robust and rustic edges for raised beds and boxing in planting. Both hardwoods and softwoods were used by rail companies over the years. Look out for reclaimed oak or tropical hardwood ties— they often come untreated, which makes them suitable for growing vegetables.*

BOOK PASSAGE

BOOKSTORE & CAFE
51 Tamal Vista Blvd.
Corte Madera
CA 94925
(415) 927-0960

BOOK PASSAGE
SAN FRANCISCO
FERRY BUILDING
(415) 835-1020

ORDER TOLL FREE
1-800-999-7909

order on the web
bookpassage.com

Garden structures

So much of what happens in the garden goes on at ground level. And yet garden structures of all kinds can be used to bring height, dramatic changes in level, and sculptural interest. But like all things in the garden, their practical purpose is also paramount. From screens to plant supports, grand obelisks to battered old doors, gardenalia has some structural surprises up its sleeve.

Wooden and wicker screens

Screens are perfect for hiding things. Whether it's a composting corner, recycling basket, a horrible fence, or an unfinished section of the garden, a screen is often used like the space under the bed—simply push things out of sight and forget about them.

But a screen can do so much more. Use two or more together and create a separate room in the garden without feeling boxed in. Site a beautiful screen in glorious isolation to draw attention to a space, rather than disguise it. Use a tall screen to provide a gorgeous backdrop for a piece of sculpture, or a squat panel to allow a glimpse of the vista beyond.

Treat it like wallpaper—use it to create pretty stage scenery for an intimate dining area or relaxing corner. Paint a wooden screen in bold colors to create a bright section of the garden or provide contrast to the planting. If it's well secured, you can even hang things from a wooden or wicker screen—invest in a few hooks and you've created an instant place to hang tools and watering cans. There is also a good practical reason to use wood or wicker screens. Wind can wreak havoc in a garden. Solid barriers, such as brick, push wind upward only for it to create faster turbulence on the other side of the wall. A wicker or slatted wooden screen, by virtue of the fact it is semipermeable, safely diffuses the wind and provides fantastic shelter for both plants and people.

OPPOSITE *Woven panels are the ultimate in green screening. Reed, willow, hazel, heather, and bamboo are all popular natural materials for weaving, providing durable and rustic partitions, backdrops, or fences for your outdoor space.*
LEFT *Wooden screens can be sculptural as well as practical. Reclaimed timber was used to create a striking background for a water feature. The planks, arranged vertically, draw the eye from the pool upward but also add an extra element of privacy and seclusion.*

Metal screens

Scrap metal has become a valuable commodity and it seems, at last, that we are starting to recognize the importance of recycling and reusing metal in all its forms. Metal screens come in all shapes and sizes, from a wide variety of sources, and can be put to use in the garden as objects of both utility and beauty. From the florid designs of nineteenth-century railings to the junkyard chic of bed springs, metal screens work well as both ornamental statements and robust frames up which to grow plants. Such screens are already visually softened by the elements and slot comfortably into outdoor use.

The options are almost limitless. Visit any reclamation yard and you'll stumble upon numerous objects that can be reinvented as a metal garden screen: balcony railings, fencing, gates, radiators, handrails, grilles, heating grates, headboards, sections of glasshouses, radiator covers, drain covers, enamel signs, reinforcing mesh, fireplace screens, window guards, and pressed tin panels. Perhaps damaged and no longer suitable for their original purpose, these architectural antiques still have value as decorative structures and garden art. Don't be afraid to experiment with objects that don't usually find their way into gardens—some of the most exciting, wonderfully eccentric spaces are made when you take an everyday item and place it in an extraordinary setting.

ABOVE *Gardens don't have to be somber. Here, recycled metal screens were used in whimsical, quirky ways to add humor and surprise to three gardens. From broken and unwanted garden tools* (LEFT) *to cast-iron headboards* (CENTER) *and rusty reclaimed mattress springs* (RIGHT)*, inspirational and creative screens can be forged from the most unpromising materials.* OPPOSITE *Sections of vintage ironwork make exceptionally pretty and practical screens. The ornate swirls and curves of these unrestored nineteenth-century examples add a touch of faded glamour and romance to this relaxed, cottage-style border.*

Doors and windows

Doors and windows are playful visual devices, but they don't often find their way into the garden. More's the pity because they can create fantastical focal points. Unlike walls and solid screens, doors and windows don't entirely close off a space. They entice the visitor to feel that there is more to explore. In symbolic terms, doors and windows are always about new journeys or adventures—this gives them an almost magical significance when used outside. When we peek through portals we may feel like an outsider looking in or an insider looking out. They are a powerful part of a designer's tool kit.

In practical terms, doors and windows can be used as screens, to partition off a special part of a garden. An open door or a clear window can frame a breathtaking vista or focal point in the distance. From a security point of view, doors and windows can block off an area to unwanted guests, while stained glass windows and door panels will bring splashes of glorious color, especially if positioned to make the most of the sun.

When using glass in the garden, it's worth just making a point about safety. Old glass is beautiful, especially when it's full of wobbles and imperfections. It's also very fragile. Children tend to crash through gardens, so it's vital you keep delicate glass at a safe height. Better still, buy safety glass film, a protective stick-on plastic coating that stops fragile glass from shattering into small pieces on impact.

OPPOSITE, ABOVE LEFT *A decorative iron panel was framed in wood, transforming it into a piece of art and an effective window, inviting the viewer to peek through to another "room" within the garden.* OPPOSITE, ABOVE RIGHT *Despite the fact this window is set within an open screen, it still helps to create the illusion of a solid wall. Only when we look again do we see the visual joke, that the fence is just as see-through as the window.* OPPOSITE, BELOW *Reclaimed windows were used here to create a piece of free-standing sculpture. Formal, geometric shapes create a bold contrast to the prairie grasses behind.* LEFT *The ingenious use of a salvaged shed facade creates a wonderful optical illusion but also serves a deeply practical purpose, connecting the garden and the woodland beyond.*

RIGHT *The rigid formal lines of a rusted iron obelisk impose discipline and form on a garden, providing counterbalance to the good-natured chaos of climbing plants.* FAR RIGHT *In contrast, this woven willow cage has become almost subsumed by the greenery it supports, seeming to grow and heave in unison with the plant as it thrives and fruits.* OPPOSITE *Salvaged lumber and sections of metal were carefully combined here to create a structure that not only offers robust support for a rigorous climber but also forms an attractive archway. Its positioning within the garden provides a clever visual link to the rural buildings behind.*

Plant supports

Climbing plants will happily attach themselves to all manner of gardenalia—gates, screens, walls, and railings—but if you want to introduce color and height right in the middle of a border, look no further than rustic plant supports.

Vintage gardenalia—from wicker obelisks to ironwork pyramids, plant spirals to simple wooden poles—bring stature and architectural grace to any garden. And whether you are growing runner beans in a pretty kitchen garden or tea roses in a formal bed, the clean lines and elegant geometry of a cone, triangle, or obelisk will contrast beautifully with the chaotic tangle of a climber.

Come the winter months, when most of the interest has gone from the garden, antique and rustic plant supports will continue to provide visual spikes and definition—a welcome break from the monotony of evergreens and empty borders. You don't even need a large yard. Plant supports work brilliantly in containers, too—simply anchor the legs firmly in potting medium and you've

created an instant framework around which climbing vegetables and flowers will happily twist and turn. Plant supports in containers also allow you to enjoy fast-growing climbers without worrying that they might take over your garden. Virginia creeper, Russian vine, honeysuckle, and certain types of clematis are vigorous bullies if allowed to romp around untamed. Kept in check in a container in a sheltered spot, they'll service you with speedy height and color.

Gazebos

When you create a garden, you always want a place from which you can sit and enjoy the fruits of your labor. For romantics at heart, nothing beats the classical refinement of a gazebo. Gazebos can be enjoyed from two perspectives. From inside, looking out, the open-sided walls of a gazebo frame different vistas. On the outside, looking in, the delicate structure is translucent, enhancing and framing the landscape, rather than obscuring it.

Beyond their purpose as places of shelter, gazebos also create handsome focal points. Many nineteenth-century examples— crafted from wirework, cast iron, and wood—are deliciously ornate, with pleasing swirls and exuberant patterns. Finer, lighter examples are also eminently portable—allowing you the freedom to shift them around the garden when the mood strikes. A vintage gazebo can create different looks. Placed at the intersection of crossing paths, or at the end of a dramatic view, a gazebo makes an imposing, formal statement. Tucked away in an overgrown corner, with a rickety bench and a pillow, it becomes the perfect cottage-garden retreat. Standing alone in an incongruous setting, it becomes a piece of sculpture.

Arches

If you want to link one part of your garden to another without making the space feel closed off, an arch always creates an elegant, welcoming gateway. Whether you source an antique wirework frame or create your own curving sculpture from scrap materials, an arch is a versatile and simple way to add stature and form. Climbing and trailing plants will curl their way up and over an arch, creating a visual feast; use scented plants and their powerful perfume will fill the air. Place arches in a sequence and you create a rewarding arcade, ideal for training vines and fruit across, or for directing visitors toward a focal point. Use an arch like a picture frame; against a wall or a hedge, it will frame a piece of sculpture or stonework.

Traditional metal arches inject a restrained, formal note into your garden. Despite their delicate construction, metal arches are surprisingly robust and can hold considerable weight, making them ideal for heavier climbers such as roses or fruiting plants. Wooden arches, by contrast, make a delightfully informal statement, especially if they are handcrafted and colonized with tiny bright blossoms or autumn foliage.

ABOVE *An antique wirework gazebo creates a cozy corner for two in this secluded spot. The open weave of these delicate garden structures makes them ideal supports for scented climbing plants such as roses, honeysuckle, and fragrant clematis, all of which will create a perfumed backdrop as you sit and while away the hours.* OPPOSITE *A large wooden gazebo nestles between thickly flowering borders and overhanging trees, breaking up the path and creating a shaded spot to stop and admire the view. Much of it is hidden during the growing season, but come winter this grand structure will provide welcome focus in a formal garden.*

RIGHT *Traditionally, arches are neat, slender structures, but this curved iron example takes the notion and turns it on its head. Imposing, rusted, and deliberately disheveled, it brings a playfully autumnal note to the space.* OPPOSITE *Interconnected wire arches create a barrel vaultedlike ceiling of climbing plants and delicate sprays. Their careful positioning also draws the eye to the focal point at the far end of the path, where a large terracotta pot sits patiently.*

Statuary and ornament

We treat gardens as an extension of our homes, so it's natural that many people choose to dress their outside spaces with statuary, urns, and other ornaments. From dramatic and captivating stone figurines to the solid elegance of iron ornaments, from the convivial heat of antique chimineas and fire pits to the reassuring trickle of a subtle water feature, whatever your choice, statuary and ornament always add a splendid air of refinement and interest.

Human figures

From kitsch cherubs to classical heroes, stone figures transfer seamlessly into the modern garden. Human statues have long been part of the vocabulary of formal gardens, but work equally well in a busy cottage garden, wildflower meadow, or urban courtyard.

Single human figures make a compelling statement. From the romantic curves of the female form to the gothic splendor of an ecclesiastical figure, human statues inject different moods depending on their type and placement. They can be melancholic, erotic, authoritative, or even humorous—it's all down to context.

Stand a lone statue next to a bench and it makes the garden feel as if it always has a visitor; place a single statue in the middle of a wide lawn and it takes on a sense of importance and drama; hide a statue among dense planting and it creates a sense of mystery and surprise.

Place a pair of human figures either side of the entrance to your plot and they act as sentries. Facing each other, they create an intimate grouping; back to back, it's a totally different statement. Group human figures in threes or more and you've got a family, a gathering, or a conversation. And, if you want to play with the traditional symbolism of statues, why not add humor to the mix? The addition of a pair of sunglasses or a top hat soon turns a stiff statue into a cheerful conversation piece.

LEFT *Statuary doesn't have to be stone. This unglazed clay bust is an unusual but elegant choice for the garden, its warm red tones blending with the surrounding pots and containers. Notoriously vulnerable to frost, however, this terra-cotta lady will probably have to spend her winters indoors.* OPPOSITE *In contrast, weathering only seems to improve the appearance of these stone figures. If your* statues haven't yet acquired the aged look, it only takes a winter for algae and lichen to begin to appear. Wait three or four years and the weathered look will have made a good start.*

RIGHT **Human statues and clipped gardens go hand in hand, but here a lone classical figure, seemingly tending the plants, is used to great effect in a rambling, wildflower space. It's a powerful and surprising juxtaposition of formal and informal elements.**

Decorative stoneware

Beyond human figures, there are numerous other forms of decorative stonework you can add to your outside space. From columns to corbels, friezes to capitals, pieces of architectural stonework can look dazzling on display. Whether tall and upright or lying picturesquely broken and abandoned, these remnants of classical buildings always add a theatrical, opulent note. Other formal elements include stone urns, birdbaths, sphinxes, benches, plinths, obelisks, and spheres. Formal decorative stonework always works well if used to punctuate a vista or placed at the far end of a path to draw the eye to a distant point.

Decorative stoneware also appeals to fans of gothic architecture. From gargoyles, grotesques, and crosses to arches and window frames, stonework from redundant or refurbished churches regularly ends in salvage yards only to be scooped up by eagle-eyed bargain hunters. Dotted around the garden, these quirky, often melancholy pieces create instant atmosphere and drama.

If you prefer your garden more rural than rarefied, there is an entire field of agricultural stonework to choose from. Both beautiful and useful, these glorious artifacts of farming history are treasured by gardeners today. Their practical origins and unfussy design make them charming, rustic additions to any garden. From millstones and animal troughs, to stone weights and cider presses, farming and agricultural collectibles are fast overtaking more formal stone elements in the garden, with prices to match.

ABOVE LEFT *Decorative stonework comes in all shapes and sizes. Here, a beautifully distressed voluted capital (the top part of a column) was cleverly repurposed into a chic seat for two.* LEFT *Landscaped grounds dotted with decorative pieces of stoneware always make a timeless, refined statement. An antique stone urn balances delicate symmetry with robust elegance.*

OPPOSITE *Staddle stones, originally used to keep granaries and haybarns raised off the ground to prevent vermin from entering, have become highly collectible pieces of gardenalia. Also known as pad or settle stones, their pleasing toadstool shape fits comfortably into any garden setting.*

OPPOSITE, ABOVE LEFT A deceptively simple network of metal pipes and watering cans has created this delightfully quirky irrigation system, which creates sparkling showers of water on demand. OPPOSITE, ABOVE RIGHT *Antique wall-mounted water spouts often started life as public drinking fountains, supplied by fresh water pumps. Today, they work just as well in a private garden, providing the soothing background noise of running water and a welcome spot for wildlife.* OPPOSITE, BELOW LEFT *Traditional cascade fountains work in both small intimate courtyards and large formal gardens. The sound and flow of gently playing water has long been associated with stress relief, as well as providing dynamic movement in an otherwise static space.* OPPOSITE, BELOW RIGHT *Water features can be child's play. This simple, domino arrangement of zinc buckets with spouts relies on gravity and a pump to constantly cycle the water down the cascade and back to the top again.* LEFT *Plastic rain barrels might be practical but they can spoil an otherwise pretty corner of your plot. This reclaimed wooden version, heavily entwined with rambling roses, makes a picture perfect alternative.*

Water features

From lead fountains to old water pumps, period water features add instant sparkle to your outside space. While classical figures and stone fountains will add an instant splash of formality, pebbles, rills, and stepped falls create a relaxed and romantic air. Stone troughs and water barrels suit the pastoral quality of a cottage garden, while cleverly converted tin baths, watering cans, and pails add a quirky touch to garden kitchens and patios.

If you're looking for a large ornate water feature, classical stoneware is a timeless option. Wall-mounted fountains with lead spouts bring a relaxing trickle to any corner of a garden, while grand centerpieces—such as figures and triple cascades—look sensational center stage in a formal setting. Even the smallest courtyard comes to life with the sound of rushing water. And whether it's a lead trough or a converted hand pump, the constant noise of crashing water provides the perfect foil for the background hum of daily life.

For a fraction of the cost of high-end statuary, you can also create water features from flea-market finds. Most large containers, as long as they are watertight, can be converted to take a water pump. From cast-iron baths to laundry tubs, animal feeders to milk churns—everything from a favorite pot to an antique showerhead can be pressed into service. Improvements in solar-powered water pumps have also removed the need for electric cabling, so you can sneak a water feature anywhere that catches the sunlight; some even store energy so your feature will flow well into the night. For more powerful water features or shady spots, however, you'll need a qualified electrician to connect the supply.

Ponds and reservoirs

Still water creates a different mood from the dynamism and excitement of a fountain or cascade. While crashing water is deeply invigorating, ponds and small reservoirs are ideal for a meditative garden and easy to create with simple pieces of gardenalia.

A tin bath or ceramic basin, a lead planter, or a large birdbath will reveal interesting reflections, ripples, and shimmers without much maintenance. Where there's water there's life, and these features are also wildlife havens, attracting birds, insects, and small mammals.

On a note of safety, both moving and still water features are hazardous for young children so it's vital that you protect areas of open water. Ponds and reservoirs can be childproofed with metal or plastic grids (netting is not strong enough), or you could build your water feature into a wall or opt for a pebble pond or tiered water feature, which doesn't pool water at the bottom.

Another challenge is to keep the water clear. Most water features—both still and moving—rely on a small self-contained reservoir. The recirculated water can soon become cloudy and smelly so it's important to remove leaves and other debris on a regular basis and consider oxygenating plants to prevent algae and bacteria from forming. You can also buy water feature and fountain tablets and solutions that tackle this problem—make sure you choose brands that are wildlife friendly.

BELOW LEFT *An oversized lead planter was press-ganged into service as a reservoir, perfect for attracting wild birds and insects and as a handy source of stored water in the drier months.*

BELOW RIGHT *Shallow dipping ponds act like mirrors, creating delicate reflections and sparkle among low-lying plants. Metal dishes were used here to create instant miniature ponds, an ideal watering hole for frogs and small mammals.*

OPPOSITE *Cattle troughs and animal feeders make excellent still water features. Robust, frost-resistant, and naturally weathered, these rural remnants look just at home in an overgrown cottage garden as they once did in a busy farmyard. Check for large cracks before you buy.*

Furniture

Nothing looks more inviting than an alfresco garden party with rustic tables, mismatched wooden chairs, twinkling candles, and comfortable benches. Outside and inside have become extensions of the same space, and there's real creativity in dressing the garden as if it were another room in the house. From junkyard sofas to exquisite wrought-iron love seats, gothic to retro-chic, when it comes to vintage and antique furniture, there is an embarrassment of riches to choose from.

Tables and chairs

The boundary between house and garden furniture is becoming unclear, but it's an ambiguity that works in our favor. Not content with horrible plastic chairs and picnic tables, many people now look toward "indoor" pieces to create relaxing spaces and entertaining areas outside in the garden. It might not seem practical to drag an upholstered armchair onto the lawn, but one of the benefits of vintage and flea-market furniture is that you don't feel too precious about the odd spot of rain or muddy handprint. If the heavens do open, most pieces are easily lifted to a sheltered spot.

The choices are dizzying. From huge industrial worktables to the molded curves of a 1960s office chair, French café seating to chunky driftwood stools, no era or style looks out of place in the garden. All budgets are catered for, too. From serious investment antiques, such as nineteenth-century cast-iron benches, to cheap and cheerful thrift store finds, it all depends on what you want to spend. The antique garden furniture market is brisk—the prices for eighteenth-, nineteenth , and early twentieth century century pieces reflect their rarity and quality. At the opposite end of the scale, junk shops, salvage yards, and flea markets are a fantastic hunting ground for mid-twentieth-century wicker, upholstered pieces, postwar furniture, and school and church benches.

OPPOSITE **Vintage dining chairs teamed with a rustic trestle table create a large and welcoming entertaining area. A chunky tabletop, crafted from heavy-duty planks, makes a beautiful, rustic, and functional surface, capable of withstanding whatever the weather will throw at it.** *LEFT* **There's no denying the inherent character and personality that comes from reusing well-worn materials in rich and inventive ways. Reclaimed matchboard was reworked here to create a solid but delicately striped armchair, perfect for a relaxing corner.** *OVERLEAF, LEFT* **Wirework chairs were combined with a heavy stone-slab-topped table to create a spare but refined look.** *OVERLEAF, RIGHT* **Metal balloon-back chairs are always a convivial choice for an entertaining area. Their café-inspired chic contrasts beautifully with the heavy-set, industrial charms of a rustic workbench.**

Statement seating

- Wooden benches provide impromptu seating for family gatherings and parties.
- A low stone bench is central to the vocabulary of a formal garden.
- A bench created from coppiced branches and prunings is testament to a resourceful gardener.
- Wirework and metal benches create instant bistro chic and work well in small courtyards.

RIGHT An ornate antique bench was matched with a vintage and well-weathered wirework armchair and simple rustic table to create a pleasing mix of nostalgic styles.

Benches

Nothing's more genial than a garden seat for two. So much of gardening is a solitary pursuit, it's nice to have a place where you can sit and share the space. As with all gardenalia, the choices of materials are vast—marble, stone, terra-cotta, wrought iron, cast iron, reconstituted stone, wood, and, with twentieth-century examples, plastic and wicker. Stone and marble can be costly and, due to their weight, will need a permanent home, while lighter benches can travel around the garden on a whim.

The positioning of your bench will also change the mood of the garden. Sit a bench in a prominent position and it can make an ideal vantage point from which to survey all your efforts. Tuck your bench in a quiet corner or underneath an overgrown arch and it becomes a hidden resting spot. Alongside a table, a bench turns from a contemplative seat into a sociable one, ready for good-natured conversation and rowdy family meals. Prop a bench by the back door and you've got the perfect place to sit and remove muddy boots. Packed with pillows and throws, a bench is instantly transformed from all-weather seating into a sofa for a sunny day.

You can also think beyond the conventional forms of garden benches. Church pews, school benches, banquettes, curved tree seats, tête-á-têtes (or conversion seats), park benches, railway benches, settles, and bar bench seats can slip seamlessly into an outdoor setting.

Recliners and deck chairs

For those of us who like to linger in the garden—glass of fizz in one hand, eyes closed, and face to the sun—nothing beats a good old-fashioned deck chair. Inherently glamorous and yet basic in design, deck chairs began life as foldaway seating for ocean liners. Back on dry land, these reclining seats soon became beach and garden favorites, and shorthand for life lived at a leisurely pace.

Most surviving deck chairs are mid-twentieth century or later, with many vintage examples still having their original, charming fabric. If the frame is sound but the canvas has perished, it's easy to unpick the upholstery tacks and quickly replace the material. Many companies now supply traditional deck chair stripes in patterns that copy both pre- and postwar designs, including narrow and broad stripes. Other collectible canvas chairs for the garden include director's chairs, folding seats with fabric canopies, hammocks, and shooting or fishing stools.

Recliners are also the perfect accessory for lounging around the garden. Some early examples are now very collectible—big-name designers such as Thonet created everything from solid oak arts and crafts recliners to light and airy bentwood chaise longues and Capri loungers. At the less expensive end of the scale, retro steel-framed camping recliners from the 1970s and 1980s can be picked up for practically no money, but add a touch of tongue-in-cheek, suburban chic to your lawn.

ABOVE LEFT *A pair of vintage folding chairs creates an intimate spot for two in this large garden. This style of chair, sometimes known as a fishing chair, is the ultimate in portable lounging, perfect for picnics and afternoon catnaps.* ABOVE RIGHT *Few pleasures are sweeter than a summer's day snoozing in a hammock. Pillows and throws add an extra dimension of coziness when the sun begins to sink behind the trees.* OPPOSITE *Deck chairs aren't just for the beach. These retro recliners are the last word in laid-back seating, their bold stripes adding a welcome splash of color to any outdoor space.*

Fire pits and chimineas

Not everything can come from the click of a switch. Compared to gas or electric heaters, nothing beats the companionable crackle of a real fire, especially when we are surrounded by family and friends.

Outdoor fires inspire intimate conversation; when the sun goes down and the evening chill creeps across the garden, we feel drawn to sit together around the flames. A campfire is always a quick option but messy and not always practical for your outdoor space. Two great alternatives are antique fire pits and chimineas. You get the pleasure of collecting branches and chopping logs, scrunching up newspaper, and making fire, without the scorched grass.

Antique fire pits are perfectly suited for the task of outdoor heating and cooking. Deliberately designed to be light and portable, and robust enough to take intense heat, your only challenge will be to decide which way the smoke is blowing. Secondhand or antique wood-burning chimineas are also a quirky vintage addition to your garden. Wood burners usually work very efficiently, but for this you need a chimney with adequate draw and to keep the stove door shut. This approach doesn't work outside, but that doesn't matter. Use an old, rusty wood-burning chiminea and keep both the door and chimney hole open—the wood will burn differently, and more quickly, but perfectly well enough for outdoor use. Wood burning chimineas are heavy and can be prone to rust, so you'll need to keep them under cover when not in use.

LEFT **Blurring the boundary between indoors and out, this garden "living room"—complete with armchair, rug, and table— is made even cozier with the companionable crackle of a wood-burning chiminea.**

Containers

From the urban window box to the rural vegetable patch, container gardening has to be one of the simplest and most satisfying ways of using gardenalia. Zinc buckets, wirework jardinières, aged stone troughs, and vintage cookie tins—almost any vessel can be transformed into a container for plants. And whether it's terra-cotta, stone, metal, or wood, there is an almost limitless variety of materials to whet your appetite.

Troughs and basins

It seems crazy to think that an item that once had such a humble, prosaic purpose has become so collectible. Most antique stone troughs started life as animal drinking or feeding vessels, well heads, or drinking fountains, but have become as valuable and sought after as fine statuary. And with good reason. Often carved by hand from solid blocks of stone, each one is unique and full of history and personality. Perfectly suited to life outdoors, stone troughs make ravishing containers for all kinds of plants, whether it's seasonal bulbs or a miniature alpine garden. Moss, lichen, and the other signs of weathering only add to their rustic appeal.

Not quite so grand, but equally versatile, vintage basins also make excellent planters. Once a common feature of the turn-of-the-century household, ceramic basins fell out of favor with the introduction of steel and plastic alternatives in the twentieth century. There is often a distinction between regional designs (some areas, being more frugal with their water supply, developed a shallower sink). Once cracked or chipped, these handsome basins are often ripped out, but many end up with a new purpose in the garden, stuffed to the brim with flowers or herbs. Most are plain or ribbed in design, but keep an eye out for ornate or unusual basins to bring a bit of period interest to your plot.

LEFT *A ceramic basin enjoys a second life as a handsome, practical planter. Note that the sink is cleverly propped off the ground on logs to allow for adequate drainage.* OPPOSITE *A huge salvaged stone basin becomes a table-height planter with the clever addition of stone supports. Stout wooden chairs create the illusion of a dining area even though this trough is now purely for plants.*

Terra-cotta containers

Reclaimed terra-cotta pots have caught the eye of shabby chic designers and gardeners, who love the feel and look of these century-old containers. In the past, these pots would have been used for everything from tomatoes to geraniums or, when displayed en masse, for auricula theaters.

They are lovely to handle and still make excellent containers—smaller thumb pots are usually rimless and great for seedlings, while bigger examples have a narrow, rounded lip and are ideal for larger plants. Victorian examples, especially if they are hand thrown or have makers' marks, have become quite collectible—you'll be able to tell whether a pot is hand thrown as you'll often see the potter's thumb prints or nail marks on the inside. Look out for pots with the producer's names still legible, as these are very collectible.

There is a huge variety of terra-cotta containers to suit all gardens and budgets. Old clay pipes are great value, for example, and make excellent plant holders—just stand them upright and fill them with trailing plants such as strawberries or pansies. Succulents and herbs will also thrive. Square terra-cotta seed pans and rectangular planters look very sweet planted up with spring bulbs or bedding plants for a cheerful and ever-changing seasonal display.

As with all collectibles, condition is key. Minor imperfections, lumps, small chips, fingerprints, bumps, and wobbles are all part of the charm of reclaimed terra-cotta. What you don't want is cracks or large chips, however, as these weaken the container, making it likely to fail under frosty conditions.

ABOVE LEFT A rich display of age-worn terra-cotta pots makes a dramatic display in this compact corner. Different-sized containers add to the pleasing clutter, making the arrangement feel spontaneous rather than contrived. ABOVE RIGHT Hand-thrown, rimless clay pots are among the prettiest and most collectible of all vintage containers, shown off to great effect in this rustic plant theater. OPPOSITE Large terra-cotta pots are a favorite of Mediterranean chateau gardens. Planted with clipped box and laurel, these geometric accents also add formality and repetition to any type of garden space.

Wooden boxes and crates

Wine crates, vegetable and fruit boxes, champagne cases, and packing crates—one person's trash is truly another person's treasure. These excellent containers are often the detritus of a busy food market but represent free and characterful containers for the salvage-savvy gardener.

Almost any size is available and can be pressed to use in the yard. Large wooden shipping crates make instant raised beds for fruit and vegetables and are ideal containers for a corner of compost. Midsized wine crates are perfect for root vegetables, which need deep soil and plenty of compost, or top-heavy, thirsty plants such as tomatoes. A shallow fruit box makes a quirky container for herbs, and looks as good on your kitchen counter

as it does outside, while individual champagne boxes stuffed with fragrant lavender create chic window boxes for a sunny ledge. Look for examples with interesting lettering, makers' names, or numbers—these add a quirky, vintage tone to your display.

On a practical note, wooden boxes and crates will need some protection from the elements if you intend to leave them outside for any length of time. A quick coat of eco-friendly exterior varnish will prolong the life of any wooden container, and you'll also need to line the inside of your container with thick plastic, pierced at the base for drainage. Not only will this protect the wood from contact with water, but it will also help the compost retain moisture and stop the plant roots from drying out.

*OPPOSITE **Scavenged wine and champagne crates make excellent containers for flowers, vegetables, and herbs. A handful of drainage holes and a quick coat of matte varnish will stop your small raised beds from becoming waterlogged and disintegrating after one season.** LEFT **Low-sided planters, such as fruit crates, apple boxes, and printers' drawers make excellent containers for shallow rooted plants and herbs. Filled with a selection of pretty pots and seedlings they also make rustic cottage-garden trays.** BELOW LEFT **Vintage wooden packing cases often come with wire-reinforced corners and handle holes, making them sturdy containers for deep-rooted plants and easy to carry around the garden planted.***

Metal containers

While wooden crates and boxes bring a soft, vintage look to your garden, if you want something a little more industrial or retro, metal containers are a sleek, stylish option. Many start life with a prosaic purpose—food tins, oil drums, jerry cans, garbage cans, chicken feeders, and flour canisters—but with a little flair and fiddling, they can be repurposed into sophisticated containers for both balconies and back gardens alike. Metal containers also have the added advantage of being frost-proof, so you don't have to worry about leaving them outside over the winter months.

Almost anything can convert to be a cool container—old cookie and food tins, milk churns, cooking pans, pots of varying shape and depth, water tanks, cutlery drainers, bread bins, enamel buckets, olive oil tins, shopping baskets, bathtubs, filing drawers, watering cans, vintage metal lunch boxes—the options are limitless and will bring a cheerful hint of humor to your planting.

Antique containers, deliberately designed for the garden, are also a chic addition to your outside space. Lead and zinc planters, hanging baskets, wirework jardinières, copper plant pots, cast-iron troughs and planters, and other collectible metal containers are a great way to display bulbs, standard trees, and plants, providing classical, formal accents around the garden.

As with all containers, drainage is essential. You'll need to drill a handful of holes into the bottom of your vessel and, if the metal isn't galvanized or precoated, you'll also need to either line it with sturdy plastic sheeting or insert a plastic tub to prevent rust forming on the inside, which can eat its way to the outer surface.

ABOVE LEFT **Metal milk churns can be planted with climbers such as clematis that will scramble over their tops.** ABOVE RIGHT *With their traditional drop handles and riveted plates, these shallow metal kadai cooking bowls have been transformed into miniature kitchen gardens.* LEFT *Old toffee tins and vintage cookie cans make a cozy cluster planted up with succulents and cacti.* OPPOSITE *Despite their prosaic origins, a reclaimed metal barrel and zinc water tank take on a sleek, refined air in this stylish backyard. The monochrome color scheme, restrained planting, and whitewashed walls help to keep the look gracefully spare.*

Wicker baskets

From hampers to shopping baskets, laundry boxes to woven pots, wicker containers are fast becoming one of the most popular ways to grow and display plants. Before the arrival of plastic, most goods were transported in wicker containers. These vintage baskets and boxes are packed with personality and can be used in imaginative, decorative ways to bring textural interest to all sorts of spaces.

Less robust than metal or terra-cotta containers, but gentler, and more organic from an aesthetic point of view, wicker baskets make ideal spring and summer planters. Wicker is prone to decay when used outside, but there are things you can do to prolong the life of a woven container. Lining the inside with thick, pierced plastic sheeting will minimize the contact of compost and container. Try not to place your wicker container directly on the ground—if you lift it slightly off the ground (using small tiles, pebbles, small sticks, and so on) this allows air to circulate beneath the container and prevents it from becoming saturated.

You can also varnish wicker, with eco-friendly lacquer, and that should give your container an extra season or two. Wicker also looks great in different colors—spray painting works more effectively than brush application, as you get an even finish over an uneven surface. One coat of primer undercoat and two topcoats will create a bright, robust basket perfect for creating a blast of color.

LEFT **Salvaged wicker baskets come from all kinds of sources. Here, old laundry baskets, still with their original numbering, were planted with vibrant hyacinths and tulips to create a dazzling display.** OPPOSITE **The rustic feel of wicker marries beautifully with the sleek lines and crisp furnishings in this modern courtyard. Wicker always blends well with other natural materials, adding an extra layer of texture and softness to the garden.**

Choice of materials
- Wooden containers such as old boxes and drawers weather beautifully but will rot if not sealed and lined with plastic.
- Leather and wicker are quirky but won't withstand protracted bad weather. Use them for spring and summer splashes of color or seasonal supplies of herbs.
- Plastic and metal containers are durable and retain moisture well.

LEFT *Reclaimed zinc baths can hold huge quantities of bedding compost, making them ideal containers for thirsty plants and deep-rooted vegetables. The tricky problem of drainage is often provided in the form of an existing plug hole.*

Recycled objects

Gardening needn't be a serious affair. When it comes to containers, you can really have some fun with flea-market finds, turning everyday objects into eye-catching displays and playful conversation pieces. Junk-shop bargains, antique planters, and whimsical collections can be cleverly combined to bring a real sense of adventure to your outside space.

When it comes to containers, almost anything goes. As long as you can fill it with enough growing medium and make a few holes in the bottom you can turn most objects into plant containers. From old suitcases to cast-iron rainwater hoppers, there is a surprising range of materials that will cope with being outside. Some, such as leather and wicker, might need extra protection

against the elements, but many others, such as plastic, stone, ceramic, wood, rubber, and metal, will cope admirably.

Think about different-sized containers, from the sublime to the ridiculous. Tiny scallop shells make exquisite little containers for succulents while cast-iron bathtubs create a bold statement, especially if they are overflowing with blousy blooms. Old leather boots or rubber boots add a touch of humor, while a broken wheelbarrow or handcart can still enjoy life outside even if it's come to the end of its original life. In the same way you would accessorize your living room, furnish your garden; mismatched vintage containers from markets, auctions, and yard sales always create a cheerful and unique decorative flourish.

Tools

Between the two World Wars a greater variety and number of garden tools were produced than at any other time. Many of these vintage implements are still quirky and collectible, which makes them charming additions to any kitchen garden or garden. Best of all, they're still perfectly useful. Apart from a very few rare or delicate survivors, most vintage tools are as ready to work now as the day they were made.

Barrows and rollers

The basic shape of gardening tools has changed little since Roman times, with only slight tweaks and refinements along the way. Before the Industrial Revolution, and its standardization, most garden implements would have been crafted by the local blacksmith or resourceful estate gardener, designed for a specific job and built to last a lifetime. With mechanization, the availability and range of tools vastly increased. The sheer variety is breathtaking—it's not unusual to find early twentieth-century tool manufacturers turning out thirty-five different types of spade and the same number of forks, including separate ones for asparagus, beetroot, and potato.

Barrows and rollers are equally diverse. One 1913 catalog lists eight different types of garden barrow, while rollers from the same period came with a variety of stone, wooden, or cast-iron cylinders depending on their price and purpose. Despite their antiquity, these handsomely robust tools still serve a useful function in the garden and also make inexpensive and attractive garden ornaments.

RIGHT *There's beauty in the sheer practical simplicity of many old tools. This sturdy vintage sack truck, also known as a dolly or a bag barrow, still has years of useful service left in it and looks totally at home propped up, ready for action.*
FAR RIGHT *The Victorians could rarely resist adding decorative flourishes to functional items. Garden rollers from this period are often embellished with ornate pierced sides and lavish makers' stamps.*
OPPOSITE *The sheer breadth of variety of vintage and antique tools is extraordinary.*

LEFT *The rusted tones and silvered wood of this vintage spade and fork create an eye-catching and sensitive piece of garden art. Tools that are long past their useful horticultural life can often still create striking wall displays and curious corners.*

Vintage and collectible tools should last a lifetime if properly looked after. You mustn't be shy about getting stuck in and putting your gardenalia to good use as you putter around the garden. Most old tools will come with a bit of grime and rust. And while you don't want to clean collectible tools so thoroughly that you remove their antique patina, all tools will require some maintenance and occasional cleaning to keep them in tip-top condition.

Most vintage tool metal is iron or steel. Given half a chance, these metals will combine with oxygen to form rust. If you are going to use vintage tools, you have to prevent these two elements getting together. The usual way is to put something on the surface that doesn't wash off easily. That means anything oily, anything waxy, or specialist sprays. None of the techniques is complicated—it's just a matter of applying, checking, and redoing as necessary.

Vintage tools also tend to have wooden handles. The wood can split, in which case it needs to be professionally mended (for a working tool) or glued together (for a decorative tool). If a wooden handle is deeply scratched or chipped, that may also need attention if you plan to use it. A damaged handle will be uncomfortable to use and should be sanded back to a usable smoothness. For a decorative tool, on the other hand, the scrapes will be part of its rustic appeal and be something to enjoy.

Beyond hand tools, there is a myriad of other vintage implements that can be pressed into use around the garden. From cloches to rhubarb forcers, watering cans to sifters, antique tools of all shapes and sizes are readily available and add instant warmth to a productive garden. While a nineteenth-century classical urn can set you back the price of a family car, the majority of tools are well within most people's budgets. Antique trowels and spades, for example, cost little more than a latte and look terrific propped up against the garden shed or hanging on a wall. Forks, watering cans, trowels, trugs, rakes, terra-cotta plant pots—all of these implements can be picked up for a song but look infinitely more beautiful than their modern counterparts.

New uses for old tools
- Use vintage watering cans and old wheelbarrows to create quirky plant containers.
- Small wooden handle tools make instant plant markers or, if slightly folded, hanging hooks for a garden shed.
- Glass cloches and bell jars make elegant outdoor chandeliers when inverted or simple table decorations for an outdoor feast.

RIGHT *Farming tools and garden implements can work particularly well displayed together. Here, a potager's paradise of terra-cotta rhubarb forcers and plant pots blends seamlessly with hand sickles, crates, and scythes.* OPPOSITE *Robust vintage hand tools often come with ash or beech handles, guaranteeing you years of character-packed use for a fraction of the cost of a modern off-the-shelf alternative.*

Garden Spaces

Kitchen gardens

Ornamental kitchen gardens are magical places. Nothing is more pleasing than a space that not only produces endless supplies of vegetables, herbs, and flowers, but also provides a feast for the senses. The best kitchen gardens succeed in transforming the simple act of growing food into something more akin to sculpture or painting—using color, shape, and quirky materials to create something of real beauty.

The influential English writer, craftsman, and social reformer William Morris once described art as "the expression by man of his joy in labour." Many of the creative things we do in our daily lives could fit this description and perhaps none so much as kitchen gardening—a task that produces results that are not only useful and hopefully delicious but incredibly beautiful too.

Gardenalia is absolutely critical to this process. Vintage tools, reclaimed salvage, and natural materials provide so many elements of what makes a kitchen garden special. Raised beds, edging, screens, paths, and fencing—these are the "bones" of an ornamental kitchen garden and give year-round structure and interest to a seasonal space. Newer, man-made materials often jar with the organic, timeless appeal of a kitchen garden. The softness and patina of recycled and secondhand materials add an instant aged feel, even to the most newly planted of plots.

The idea of kitchen gardens is an old one, so it seems appropriate that we should encourage all things antique, collectible, and vintage into their design. Even as far back as the twelfth century we have clear evidence of this type of garden—there is a famous plan of Canterbury Cathedral from around 1150 showing a herbarium that provided plants for both medicine and cooking. In these early ornamental gardens, plants were grown either in woven containers or pots or in square or rectangular raised beds edged with planks. Rows of vegetables were fenced with trellis, palings (fences made from pointed sticks), or wattle, all of which transform seamlessly into a twenty-first-century kitchen garden.

PREVIOUS PAGES *A design classic, the vintage Model A chair has been popular since the 1930s. Crafted from sheet metal, it's not only sleekly handsome but very light and remarkably tough, making it the perfect outdoor chair.* LEFT *The practice of creating rows of raised beds using woven containers dates back to medieval monastery gardens but still works perfectly in a modern kitchen garden.* OPPOSITE *The pure pleasure that comes from growing and eating your own produce is only enhanced by making a formal, ornamental kitchen garden. Here, reclaimed boards have created neat, square beds.*

Beds are the building blocks of a kitchen garden. Raised beds work well for so many reasons: they control the excesses of vigorous plants, make harvesting and weeding easier, clearly separate paths and produce, and, most of all, create pleasing formal shapes and the reassurance that the garden is well and truly under control.

To create raised beds, the walls need to be strong enough to take a substantial weight of soil. Railroad ties are a speedy, solid option and reclaimed bricks make a pretty, durable dwarf wall, especially if you can source bricks to match existing exterior walls.

If you prefer ground-level beds, a simple visual tool is to edge with a solid line of bricks, pavers, or cobbles. Wicker hurdles, dwarf picket fences, shuttering (thin planks laid horizontally, long edge downward), Victorian rope-edge tiles, and glass bottles also work well for demarcating growing spaces.

In a productive kitchen garden, gardenalia can also provide an important supporting role. Many edible plants are climbers, or need support to help them grow. From wicker obelisks to cast-iron wigwams, wrought-iron screens to hazel pea-sticks, vintage and natural materials provide sturdy yet attractive support for everything from sweet peas to runner beans. Fruit trees and shrubs also need to be trained, and whether you create a reclaimed brick wall for an espaliered apple or driftwood raspberry canes, salvaged materials will look better than modern, plastic counterparts.

ABOVE *A formal kitchen garden with a twist. Look closer and we see workaday, modest materials such as railroad ties and recycled bricks transformed by being used in such an elegant manner.* OPPOSITE *Using gardenalia at different heights creates visual spikes and interest in this cottage kitchen garden. From scarecrows to wicker edging, cane toppers to wigwams, each element adds a layer of complexity and form to this fruitful plot.*

Vegetables often need cosseting over the winter or a gentle shove in spring. In a kitchen garden there are a number of portable ways gardeners can protect and encourage vulnerable plants.

Introduced by the Victorians to cover plants and extend the growing seasons, cloches have an enduring vintage appeal. Some of the earliest cloches are the simple glass bell jars, designed to pop over individual plants. For rows of plants that needed protection, antique "barn cloches" became a handsome alternative—these tentlike cloches can be used by themselves or arranged in a straight line. Other pretty cloches are the highly collectible cast-iron "handlights" that resemble tiny Victorian greenhouses.

Woven cloches provide a softer, more organic look than glass. Despite their open weave, they do give plants a small amount of protection against light frosts. In really bad weather they need to be lined with straw or newspaper for extra insulation, but for most of the year woven cloches provide attractive and much-needed defense against troublesome pests and strong winds.

Forcers also offer dots of interest around the vegetable plot, although they promote plant growth by excluding light, rather than encouraging it. In a large kitchen garden, both cloches and forcers can look rather lost if displayed in isolation—try grouping them in odd numbers or creating neat rows.

These kitchen garden favorites also transfer well to outdoor entertaining. Glass cloches work brilliantly used as food covers or simple table decorations. Hung upside down and filled with candles, they also make elegant outdoor chandeliers.

ABOVE RIGHT **Antique glass cloches or bell jars protect tender seedlings from the worst of the weather and also add sparkle and reflection to your kitchen garden. They make the strongest visual statement arranged in rows, helping to define a space or separate two areas of crops.**

RIGHT **Vintage woven cloches might look delicate but they are more than capable of withstanding the elements and blend naturally with the garden, offering protection from predators and pinching frosts.**

LEFT *Old terra-cotta forcers with mismatched tops—used for encouraging earlier, sweeter crops of rhubarb and chicory— look sensational in any style of kitchen garden, adding buttons of interest to any planted patchwork.*

Decoration

- Small decorations work best in families of three or more.
- Rows and symmetry create a formal kitchen garden, while clusters and odd numbers lend an informal note.
- Decorations need to be beautiful *and* useful—kitchen gardens are ultimately practical spaces.
- For a true kitchen garden add wooden spoon plant markers, glass bottles, and blackboards.

LEFT *Scarecrows are not only practical in a vegetable plot, keeping hungry birds away from seeds and young shoots, but also add sculptural interest and a note of kitsch humor.*

Beyond the serious business of protecting plants, decorative gardenalia can bring a kitchen garden to life, adding humor, originality, and flashes of eccentricity. The devil's in the detail, so look for small attractive items that can be dotted around your plot. Canes can be dangerous for your face or eyes when you bend over, but there are lots of quirky ways to top them. Try small plant pots, seashells, decorative cans, pebbles, or terra-cotta pots.

Plant markers are another rich seam for quirky ideas. Reclaimed slate roof tiles, children's chalkboards, wooden spoons, river rocks, lollipops, corks on sticks, hazel twigs, driftwood, razor clam shells, and old tool handles create free or low-cost labels. Antique hunters can also find Victorian terra-cotta and slate examples or vintage tin and zinc plant markers, or "tallies" as they are sometimes known.

When it comes to managing the wildlife, gardenalia also has lots to offer the canny kitchen gardener. Homemade bee and bug houses will attract insects of all shapes and sizes—from upturned terra-cotta pots filled with straw or scrunched-up newspaper to tiny wooden houses, these miniature residences are ideal for enticing welcome wildlife. Vintage and handcrafted bird boxes are also perfect for a kitchen garden—wild birds eat a vast number of pests, weed seeds, and sometimes even small rodents. For the birds you don't want, you can always call on the services of a scarecrow. Kitsch and sculptural, a reclaimed or homemade bird scarer will look fantastic, whether placed among dense planting or guarding a newly sown crop. For an extra retro touch, dress your scarecrow in pretty vintage clothing from a thrift store.

The orchard

Orchards and heritage apple varieties, in particular, are enjoying a huge revival. More and more of us are waking up to the pleasure of growing and picking our own fruit and the experience is made even sweeter when you use antique tools and equipment. From bushel baskets to apple crates, wooden trugs to willow apple pickers, there's a lovely variety of specialized, vintage gardenalia.

Traditional orchard ladders, for example, have three legs to make it easier to reach the trickiest branches and look fantastic propped against a tree. Out of season, these slender ladders also make excellent bathroom towel holders or rails for hanging storage.

Old-fashioned apple storage racks, with their slatted wooden drawers, provide plenty of space to store neat rows of fruit. Rustic yet elegant, these simple drawers also make handy storage for other garden and household basics. Wooden apple trays work equally well in the garden shed for rows of small pots or create instant shelving wherever it's needed. Wicker harvest baskets and enamel buckets make lovely, country-style containers for everything from fresh produce to container plants, while vintage crates or "bushel boxes" make stylish storage or growing boxes around the garden.

Apple presses have changed little over the years so a vintage example could easily be brought back into service. Even those that have finished their useful life still make great garden art and can be converted into plant containers or water features.

ABOVE LEFT Reproductions of nineteenth- and early twentieth-century enamel buckets are now commonplace, proving that good, simple design is timeless. Enamelware has reemerged as a popular choice both indoors and around the garden, and is an essential ingredient for the farmhouse country look.
LEFT Orchard ladders have three legs for stability and a tapered body to allow the fruit picker easy reach to the most difficult areas of the tree.

OPPOSITE Gardenalia can transform the simple act of fruit harvesting into a vintage-packed pleasure. Here, a rustic table and chair, complete with antique enamelware and a vintage flask, provide a much-needed break from the hard work of apple collecting.

An Artist's Palette

What happens when you cross a gardener with an artist? The answer is evident in Jo Campbell's sumptuous kitchen gardens. Originally trained as a fine artist, Jo's painterly eye and sculptor's flair inform every garden she creates, and the results are as pleasing to the eye as they are to the palate.

Thanks to her confident use of color and form, combined with an encyclopedic knowledge of edible plants, Jo Campbell has become one of the most accomplished and creative vegetable gardeners in the United Kingdom, creating exquisite kitchen gardens for both Michelin-starred restaurants and private clients alike. But perhaps the most characteristic feature of Jo's gardens is her clever use of gardenalia. From the initial design to the everyday tasks, Jo incorporates reclaimed materials, garden collectibles, and vintage tools into her planted patchworks. And whether it's reclaimed herringbone walkways or roof-tile edging for paths, Jo understands the importance of choosing materials that complement both the house and the rest of the garden.

Changes in height provide three-dimensional interest—tall willow obelisks, arches, and hazel sticks reach skyward and give a wonderful contrast to the dense, low rows of flowers and vegetables. Sculpture also adds a visual twist to many of Jo's garden creations, bringing life and movement.

Natural materials play a huge part in the design process. Whether it's hazel hurdles, willow planters, timber logs, or cleft oak edging, Jo's use of local materials not only gives the garden a vernacular flavor but also provides employment for local craftspeople and artists. Basket makers and willow weavers make her raised beds and herb planters, while a local potter provides an army of rhubarb forcers and cane toppers, which are both simple and beautiful. They also make the garden totally custom-made, adding variety year after year, and between gardens.

Gardenalia plays its part even in the smallest details—trugs and baskets, chalkboards, enamel florists' buckets, wasp catchers, labels, hand tools, and containers—each handmade, unique, or chosen for its ability to show off Jo's produce to the best effect. Her obsession with color and form feed into the display of the produce even once it's picked. Baskets overflow with neatly tied bundles of beans, while brightly stemmed chard and multicolored beetroot look as tempting and vivid as hard candy. At no stage, however, does gardenalia threaten to overtake the garden and outshine the real stars of the show—the plants. Jo's skill is knowing how to create structure and backdrop, a canvas onto which she can apply the seasonal colors of flowers and vegetables. Any decorative object found in the garden has to work hard too—practicality is equally important as looks when it comes to Jo's choices of garden features.

PAGE 98 *Kitchen gardens don't come more decorative or delicious. Sweet peas and French beans twist around native silver birch and hazel twigs, while terra-cotta planters jostle for space among rows of flowers and vegetables.* PREVIOUS PAGE, ABOVE LEFT *A motley crew of reclaimed containers from chimney pot to wine crate, assembled with Jo's natural flair, are transformed into a charming herb corner.* PREVIOUS PAGE, ABOVE RIGHT *Jo's innovative approach to vegetable gardening also feels wonderfully familiar. Her formal layouts and neat rows of vegetables are reminiscent of children's storybook gardens, pleasing in their symmetry and neatness.* PREVIOUS PAGE, BELOW LEFT *Never far from her artistic training, Jo is always keen to use wicker sculpture as a whimsical focal point.* PREVIOUS PAGE, BELOW RIGHT *Woven hurdles, commissioned from a local craftsman, add a textured backdrop to Jo's companion planting.* OPPOSITE *Jo's choice of gardenalia is timeless— natural materials and reclaimed objects bring such a sense of nostalgia to her kitchen garden, a Victorian vegetable gardener would feel instantly at home with her heritage varieties and age-old techniques.*

The Priory Garden

Monastery gardens were traditionally self-sufficient, producing fruit, vegetables, and herbs for both cooking and healing. They also used hurdles, woodwork, raised beds, and fences to create quiet, enclosed spaces full of symbolism. Taking inspiration from medieval tapestries and manuscripts, the owners of the twelfth-century Prieuré d'Orsan in France have created a garden that is both deeply spiritual and life sustaining.

PREVIOUS PAGES, LEFT **Wooden lattices support vines. Woven structures play a pivotal role in this medieval-inspired garden, demonstrating the age-old art of wood weaving or "tressing."** PREVIOUS PAGES, RIGHT **Exquisite but impermanent, all the woven seats, arches, trellis, and raised beds require constant maintenance from the head gardener and his team.** ABOVE **Basket work creates raised beds in the vegetable and herb gardens, as well as providing robust support for bright squashes.** OPPOSITE, LEFT **Fragrant climbers soon colonize the wigwams and obelisks, embracing and covering these simple but elegant frameworks.** OPPOSITE, RIGHT **Reclaimed oak boards, edged with hand-woven dwarf hurdles, create a gentle curved walkway through blanket beds of cabbages.**

In a quiet corner of the Loire Valley there's a little slice of heaven. When you gaze at the magnificently restored buildings and monastery garden at the Prieuré d'Orsan, it's hard to imagine it was once just a group of derelict buildings and neglected land. And yet it was due to the determination, vision, and hard work of architect owners Patrice Taravella and Sonia Lesot, with the help of head gardener Gilles Guillot, that this unpromising space was restored into a mecca for serious gardeners.

The space is divided into different enclosures reminiscent of a monastery garden. These include a herbarium for growing culinary and medicinal plants, a berry path, olive grove, orchard, vegetable plot, and, at the heart of the garden, a green cloister with a fountain. Each "room" is connected by leafy passages of rose

arches, espalier fruit trees, and pleached hornbeam. It's a formal garden, neatly clipped and pleasing in its geometry, but it's also an exciting space, one that uses natural materials, objets trouvés, and salvage in the most extraordinary ways.

Most characteristic of all is the garden's widespread use of wood-tressed sticks. From fences to benches, gates to edges, trellis to plant supports, coppiced twigs are twisted, plaited, and contorted to create architectural structures around the garden. They also form raised beds for the vegetable garden, individual planters, bird boxes, forcers, arches, arbors, and occasional seating.

Elsewhere around the garden, Chenin grapevines scramble up handmade willow frames, climbers wind their way around wigwams, and wooden screens mark the edge of the garden's

boundaries. Small touches of gardenalia are everywhere, too—pairs of semicircular roof tiles are lashed together to create containers for growing carrots, while small slate signs make pretty plant markers.

Around the plot, areas of decking and paths are made from reclaimed railroad ties and old oak floorboards, while the impressive fountain at the center of the cloister garden was built, by Patrice and Sonia, from reclaimed stone. Other troughs and basins, also salvaged from the building site, are dotted around.

Vintage gardens

With most garden styles, there is a clear set of rules. We know formal gardens need straight lines and symmetry; cottage gardens should be overflowing, energetic, and full of rustic charm. But what about vintage spaces? With such a pick-and-mix style surely the rule is "there are no rules"? Well, not exactly.

Never has there been a design style that takes so much effort to appear effortless. And yet, when it's done with flair and skill, it creates some of the most exciting, individual, and charismatic outdoor spaces. Vintage gardens are packed with personality, humor, and warmth. They take the best of the past and bring it into the present, using a clever combination of twentieth-century finds to create contrast and visual quirks.

At first glance, vintage garden decor looks like it's been spontaneously thrown together. And while it's important to keep that element of relaxed, unfussy styling, there are some definite tricks to designing and decorating with thrift store finds and twentieth-century treasures to ensure pleasing results.

The first rule is to choose items that are old but not too old. Anything over one hundred years old would be classed as an antique, anything less than twenty years old is too recent. "Vintage" covers that diverse and rapidly changing period between these two extremes and embraces everything, including 1960s retro, 1970s kitsch, junk-shop finds, country bric-a-brac, modern classics, and industrial chic.

The second rule of vintage is to have nothing that is too precious or valuable. The very essence of vintage style is to find beauty in items that other people class as redundant junk or too old-fashioned. Vintage gardens should be relaxed, easygoing places—who cares if something gets scratched or marked? It's all part of the history and life of a piece. Rust, peeling paint, dents, and scrapes all add to this feeling of nostalgia and the passage of time. A particularly battered piece of furniture might be too shabby for life indoors but can still enjoy its retirement out in the garden.

LEFT *Greater than the sum of its parts, a secondhand table, wooden milk crate, trio of wasp catchers, and shabby woven basket combine to create vintage alchemy in this quietly rustic corner.* OPPOSITE *Vintage café chairs and tables, painted in a pleasing palette of lollipop shades, are both delicate and surprisingly robust, perfect for a woodland picnic or impromptu meal under the stars.*

Rule three is to mix and match. Vintage chic is the antithesis of contemporary, coordinated living. Each piece of furniture or decoration should have an individual personality of its own. Vintage items should feel as if they've been amassed over a lifetime, one by one—a chair here, a pillow there. Part of the pleasure of vintage decoration is the idea you've discovered treasures in unpromising places—nothing's more thrilling than picking up bargains in a scruffy flea market or lifeless thrift store. Grouped together, these furniture "misfits" create wonderful visual contrasts; the differences in each piece are brought into relief when placed against a contrasting style or texture. That's why a metal café chair looks so fantastic next to a rustic wooden table or a softly upholstered armchair. You are creating an exciting dialogue between differing aesthetics. Different items of the same material can also look sensational grouped together—glass bottles of different heights, colors, and ages look fantastic en masse, for example, or a diverse collection of ornamental architectural ironwork.

Rule four: Don't take it too seriously. Vintage style should have a sense of humor. Some of the most enjoyable gardens use vintage items to create cheerful corners or visual surprises. Items that were overly sentimental, risqué, unfashionable, or staid in their day can create gentle humor and nostalgia when reemployed in a modern garden—a bad-tempered public notice, for example, or a kitsch figure can create a chuckle in the right context.

Rule five: Find new uses for old things. Vintage is the greenest of garden styles, taking other people's junk and turning it into riches. From packing crates to café furniture, trestle tables to medicine bottles—there's a rich seam of vintage finds to be mined.

OPPOSITE *Clever layers of vintage goodies create homespun charm. From heirloom fabrics to florists' buckets, wooden crates to wirework details, this pretty set creates a cozy corner for one.*
ABOVE RIGHT *There is elegance in everyday items. Vintage and secondhand glass bottles make gorgeous displays grouped in* odd numbers and filled with seasonal sprigs or candles.
RIGHT *An outdoor basin with vintage attitude. Sponged enamelware, zinc watering cans, and terra-cotta pots look terrific huddled around this galvanized basin. Industrial basins, rescued from salvage yards, make practical and quirky wash areas for the resourceful gardener.*

RIGHT *A driftwood sideboard creates a nicely neutral surface for a display of vintage and homemade treasures. From tealights to trinkets, birdcages to twigs, there is real charm and charisma in this magpie's collection.* OPPOSITE *Gardenalia in the greenhouse. A reclaimed ceramic basin makes a handy spot for washing vegetables and flower arranging. Vintage metal downlighters, a salvaged brick floor, and yards of quirky shelving make this a useful but undeniably characterful space.*

Artistic touches

- Have fun with everyday domestic items. Fill them with plants or use them in a display of wall art.
- Find beauty in the craftsmanship of industrial salvage—reclaimed cast-iron grilles, for example, can be highly decorative.
- Create visual jokes with signage, lettering, or advertising plaques.
- Be selective—groups of similar objects create strong visual effects.

LEFT *An old school locker gets a second life as a garden store cupboard. The battered paintwork and missing door only add to the life story of such a piece, lending real personality to an outdoor space.*

In a vintage mindset, nothing is redundant—reclaimed school lockers become handy garden storage, old wooden milk crates make rustic wine bottle holders, wirework birdcages transform into garden chandeliers, and chipped teacups make charming containers for spring bulbs or tealight holders for outdoor entertaining.

And finally, don't be afraid to lavish love and attention on a vintage find to bring it back into use. There's a fine line between shabby chic and scruffy garden, so clean and repair anything that's broken or unusable. Some vintage gardenalia will look better given a smart new coat—don't be worried about respraying or painting dull furniture with bold colors or stains. Certain things look better stripped back to their original metal or wood. Others improve with a lick of varnish. Replace very tatty fabric and upholstery—dining chair seat-pads, for example, are easy to re-cover with just a small piece of fabric and a staple gun. In a vintage garden, things have to be practical as well as pretty.

When trash and treasure are two sides of the same coin, how do you stop your outdoor space looking like a junkyard? Aficionados of vintage will tell you that, far from being a "throw it all together and see what works" process, vintage is all about what you don't include. It's all in the editing. Decorating with vintage has been compared to packing a suitcase to go on holiday—put everything you've got together and then start taking things away until you've got the core essentials. Some pieces of vintage are so spectacular or unusual, for example, they work best in isolation. A fantastically weathered arbor or retro hanging seat, for example, needs space to show off. Other vintage finds look better in a group. Spontaneous, eclectic collections can look sensational, but if you want to avoid the rummage-sale look, keep the surrounding plants and hard landscaping simple. Too much pattern and busy planting will soon turn a quirky space into a chaotic one.

Bohemian Backyard

Decadence, theatricality, and glittering treasures—in the minute backyard of her London vintage clothes shop, Virginia Bates has created a timeless treasure trove, bursting with antique gardenalia, sparkle, and joyful irreverence.

Every girl loves her dressing-up box. So why should you have to give it up just because you're all grown up? Virginia Bates' exquisite and remarkable shop is overflowing with delicate antique clothes and vintage costume, perfect for all of us who need to indulge in a touch of make-believe now and again. But tiptoe out of the back of the shop and the fantasy continues.

Out of her "little yard of nothing," as Virginia once described it, a magical space has been formed, dressed to the nines with flamboyant fabrics, ostrich feathers, and ornate chandeliers. The walls are painted candy-store pink, the perfect backdrop for a vintage over-mantel mirror and antique French café table. A 1930s floral shawl makes a pretty and impromptu tablecloth while little shelves and surfaces, accessorized with single pots and collected containers, create floor-to-ceiling splashes of color.

On the floor, a butterfly mosaic, created by artist friend Jo Ortmans, dazzles like a huge vintage brooch, while an old wirework etagere provides a theatrical stage for an ever-changing cast of pink and green hydrangeas, busy Lizzies, and petunias in old terra-cotta. A well-established pot of jasmine has settled in nicely, quickly colonizing the doorway, climbing down into the basement and artfully entangling itself into an old birdcage.

Like putting together a fantastic outfit, dressing the backyard with vintage gardenalia involved the same deft touch and eye for sparkle. A simple backdrop was brought to life with glittering accessories, quirky accents, and subtle tones. It's a testament to what can be created with vintage finds and flair, even in the smallest and most unpromising of outside spaces.

But it doesn't stop there. Away from the shop and back in the comfort of her own garden, Virginia's passion for antique gardenalia and romantic garden dressing continue apace. From wirework chairs to reclaimed tiles, hanging chandeliers to stained glass treasures, it seems there's always something magical happening at the bottom of this garden.

Gardenalia embodies the very essence of garden dressing. Rather like a sparkly necklace or bright scarf can breathe life into a plain outfit, garden collectibles and pretty pots provide those deft touches that transform a dull, lifeless space into an outdoor haven full of dynamic decoration and vintage bling. What's more, you can chop and change your choices as often as you like, reviving your decorations from season to season as you do with your flowers.

OPPOSITE *The risers of these outside steps have been adorned with a hodgepodge of vintage ceramic tiles, creating a pretty patchwork of colors and patterns.* LEFT *Ornate wirework chairs, a rusted chandelier, rambling pink roses, and a blousy shawl tablecloth make perfect vintage partners, put together with Virginia's trademark bohemian flair.* OVERLEAF, LEFT *The courtyard is bursting with vintage treasures; every wall and surface are lovingly stuffed with garden antiques, distressed materials, and floral accents. Bespoke touches, such as the butterfly mosaic, help create a truly unique space.* OVERLEAF, RIGHT *In her unmistakably feminine and theatrical garden, Virginia's wirework jardinière makes a show-stopping stage for a troop of pink blooms.*

Vintage Entertaining

Few things are more pleasurable than a meal under the stars. But for many of us the weather is a fickle friend and can soon spoil our best-laid plans. The solution? An alfresco garden room with a cleverly disguised canopy and plenty of vintage character.

It can be difficult to create a space that truly blurs the boundary between outside and in. And yet this organic entertaining space does just exactly that. What could have been an unprepossessing patio was transformed into a natural *en plein air* haven thanks to a seamless combination of architectural and natural elements.

Above of the dining space is a simple, robust structure. The uprights, despite being stark, white iron columns, have become colonized with creeping vines and climbers, helping them to blend almost invisibly into the background. Finding their way up the columns and onto the roof, these trailing plants also create dappled shade and a gentle green ceiling onto which antique birdcages have been ingeniously hung in nests of odd numbers. For all its abundance, the planting is deceptively simple. Plenty of muted green tones to provide an unfussy background to the real showstoppers—the vintage collectibles and flea-market finds.

The vintage theme continues in the choice of table and seats. A rustic pine country table makes a sturdy but elegant dining surface, complemented by a generous selection of distressed, wirework chairs, which add an instant touch of café-culture chic.

It's a space that's both fanciful and delicate. Slender-legged pot stands, ornate candelabra, and slim bentwood chairs create an old-fashioned, distinctly feminine look, tempered by the inclusion of rotund garden ornaments and heavy terra-cotta planters. Patina is important here, too. From the flaking paintwork on the café chairs to the well-worn stone pavers on the patio floor, almost every surface is marked by the passage of time and from being exposed to the ravages of the elements.

But there's also a dry sense of humor at work. The contrast of empty birdcages and pottery pigeons makes a visual pun for anyone who's battled with greedy garden birds. Vintage throws, antique rugs, and a scattering of antique children's toys finishes the playful, slightly dreamlike look of this gorgeous, green garden room.

PREVIOUS PAGES, LEFT **Vintage dining at its most sophisticated, a battered country table surrounded by chic café chairs invites guests to sit and linger over lunch.** PREVIOUS PAGES, RIGHT **Collectible birdcages hang from the green overhead canopy like delicate lampshades, adding to the illusion of an indoor dining space.** OPPOSITE, LEFT *Three vintage soda siphons in emerald green shades make a quirky but quietly effective table decoration.* OPPOSITE, RIGHT *A bentwood antique recliner, softened with an opulent throw, promises lazy afternoons spent snoozing in the shade.* RIGHT *Iron gardenalia in its many forms. From the delicately twisted wrought-iron bistro seating to finely detailed plant stands, cast-iron candelabra to sturdy metal boundary fencing—all weathering beautifully in this exquisite indoor/outdoor space.*

Formality and order

As garden writer Ursula Buchan once wrote, "Like middle-aged women everywhere . . . gardeners still extol the virtues of good bone structure." In other words, however blousy and energetic your planting scheme, the best gardens always have a strong skeleton underneath them. Take a good bone structure, enhance it with carefully chosen pieces of gardenalia, and you've got the formula for an exciting, elegant formal garden, regardless of its size or position.

Nature is chaotic, or at least it seems that way. For hundreds, if not thousands, of years gardeners have been trying to tame nature by creating formal gardens. The first garden picture, found in an Egyptian tomb dated to around 1475 BC, shows a simple formal courtyard of lotus flowers, date, and sycamore trees. Formality continued to be popular throughout the centuries that followed—from the ornamental kitchen gardens of medieval monasteries to the classical French gardens of Louis XIV—and their neat lines and pleasing proportions still appeal today. Plants run riot if left to their

RIGHT *A pair of cherubs creates order and balance. Whether it's mirror images or repetitions of the same shape, formal gardens play on the fact that people find symmetry not only aesthetically pleasing but also deeply reassuring.* OPPOSITE *Reflections are another way to create symmetry. The still water of a rill or shallow pond will act as a mirror, doubling the impact of any statue or garden structure you place near it.*

own devices—formal gardens have long been a way of people attempting to stamp their authority over nature by controlling it into neat sections. Unkempt or wild spaces are simply too lawless for some gardeners—by hemming in plants and rigorously dividing up spaces we can create harmony, balance, and pleasing predictability.

We are naturally drawn to formality. The ancient Greeks believed that symmetry is an important ingredient in our judgment of what's beautiful. Modern science proved them right—we now know humans equate physical symmetry with biological fitness; it seems we're programmed to find proportion more attractive. We instinctively know if a space feels lopsided, unequal, or unbalanced.

There are compelling practical reasons for creating a formal layout in your garden. Formal designs work brilliantly in both large and small gardens—even the tiniest urban backyard suits a design based on mathematical shapes. Circles, squares, crosses, rectangles, and ellipses—these horizontal elements provide a sense of serenity and order, especially when contrasted with prolific and generous planting. Formality can also help you make a bold statement, providing elements of surprise and visual interest but in a tightly controlled way. Of course, the larger the garden the more of a statement you can create—nothing is more captivating than landscape gardens with sweeping vistas punctuated with statues, follies, and other ornamental stonework.

Formal gardens also sit comfortably with traditional architecture. Most houses follow rules of balance and symmetry; a geometric garden is a way to unite house and garden. Some of the most successful garden schemes have a defined structure near the house, with more informal elements creeping in as you move further away.

RIGHT **Sections of prairie-style planting or wildflowers often feature in formal gardens, providing a witty contrast to their manicured surroundings. Control and structure are never far from hand, however. This patch of meadow planting is visually curtailed by four large clipped topiary balls and a formal stone urn in the center.**

ABOVE *Iron gates make a classical statement in this grand walled garden. Set between two high columns, this slender but secure opening creates a theatrical focal point but also permits glimpses of the vista beyond.* OPPOSITE *In formal gardens, sundials are often placed at the axis of four walkways. The sundial in this garden is also cleverly aligned with the gazebo in the backdrop, drawing the eye down the narrow path, between the sumptuous beds and into the distance.*

Gardenalia plays a vital role in creating formality and order. Structure doesn't just come from the plants, walls, trees, and hedges, but also in the form of fences, trellises, pergolas, statuary, paths, and water features. You can create ordered beds using salvaged edging or statues and figures to provide whimsical or arresting focal points. Obelisks and columns can be employed to lend symmetry, while garden buildings such as gazebos, summerhouses, and pergolas are elegant additions for creating formalized growing spaces or relaxing areas.

Sundials, arbors, reclaimed ironwork, and even salvaged doors and windows will help build a formal-style garden that takes reference from the past but lives in the present. Placed in the garden all year round, these permanent pieces of gardenalia offer consistency and form whatever the weather, acting as a backdrop to the ever-changing seasons and plants. Certain gardenalia—statues, urns, fountains— can bring a stately glamour or exotic refinement to our gardens. A beautiful statue is as captivating as hundreds if not thousands of pounds worth of planting and will only improve with age.

When you are incorporating gardenalia into an outside space, a number of devices always work well: reflections, for example, can double the appeal of a piece of ornamental stonework. Statuary, in particular, looks fantastic displayed at the edges of ponds—the water acts as a mirror and the effects can be enchanting.

Formal gardenalia can be used to draw the eye to a breathtaking view or secret corner. Placed at the end of an avenue or path, a stone statue or urn will visually lengthen the view. Placed in the middle of a plot, the same piece will shorten the space, making it feel more intimate but with an innate sense of drama. Hide a piece of statuary around a hedge or in the shade of a tree, and you've added a sense of playfulness, mystery, or surprise.

Formality also helps us make sense of a landscape. The rigid lines and clean shapes of a formal garden contrast beautifully with the natural undulations of a hillside or the unkempt backdrop of a forest. It's no surprise that some of the best formal gardens work because they are deliberately designed to provide an exhilarating contrast with their rugged surroundings. Even just a hint of formality, within a more relaxed planting scheme, can provide a welcome change of pace—it's exciting to see a classical figure within a cottage garden, for example, or an iron obelisk plant support at the back of an overflowing vegetable bed.

French Dressing

Formal gardens and antique gardenalia have enjoyed a long and fruitful relationship. Following in the footsteps of centuries of tradition, Dominique Lafourcade uses timeless classics to bring an elegant Provence garden to life.

PREVIOUS PAGES, LEFT **A columned walkway stands its ground against a rich backdrop of mature trees and neat topiary.** PREVIOUS PAGES, RIGHT **Soldier-straight wooden struts cast pleasing shadows on the gravel drive. The gate's gently undulating shape provides a familiar echo of the Provençal hills beyond.** ABOVE LEFT **A rustic blue gate picks up the color of the ancient shutters beyond, making the outside space feel like an extension of the house.**

ABOVE RIGHT **Terra-cotta pots can look lost displayed in isolation. Here, Dominique uses an ornate plant stand to create a dense, interest-packed arrangement of individual plants.** OPPOSITE, LEFT **An armillary sphere makes a sculptural centerpiece to this formal garden room, the view beautifully framed by a living arch.** OPPOSITE, RIGHT **In a dry landscape, water features take on extra significance. This stunning stone trough creates an oasis.**

A year in Provence can be tough on a gardener. Between chilly winters and baking hot summers, there's barely enough time to get your breath back before being battered by spring floods and violent winds. That doesn't deter self-taught garden designer, Dominique Lafourcade, however. With an architect's eye and a love of Renaissance gardens, she has created some of her country's most exclusive and exquisite outside spaces.

Her approach is clear: "A garden is first and foremost a work of art, with the gardener playing the roles of architect, sculptor, musician, and painter in turn. A garden should move visitors, setting all their senses aquiver." But how do you create such an impressive, stimulating space when all the elements are against you?

The answer is to start with structure and form—the architecture of the garden. Inspired by historical gardens, Dominique creates

lines of perspective, areas of contrast and changing levels using the familiar tools of formal gardenalia. Stone terraces, terra-cotta pots, water features, statuary and sculptures, arbors, and trellises all provide points of interest. It's a constant balancing act between straight lines and curves, geometry and natural forms.

Patios and gravel-covered surfaces, dotted with furniture, create relaxed outdoor entertaining areas—perfect for an alfresco meal. Large terra-cotta pots bring welcome splashes of color in a predominantly green space, while clipped topiary is arranged in pairs and pleasing groups. As in many formal gardens, repetition is a vital device. From rows of plants in pots to avenues of cypress trees, stone column walkways to lines of lavender—there's strength in numbers. It's a practical approach, too; a limited choice of plants will survive a scorching summer, so it's essential to repeat what works.

The house and its outside space are two halves of a whole. Provence gardens have always made the most of the gentle backdrop created by a rustic farmhouse or chateau. The brightly painted wooden shutters and doors contrast brilliantly with the muted palette of Mediterranean plants. Terra-cotta pots blend seamlessly with the sun-bleached facades of buildings, while rustic stone fountains and troughs offer relief from the dry summers and hint at the agricultural landscape beyond. It's a technique that's worked for hundreds of years and still looks dazzling today.

Regal Formality

Almost a decade ago, Jan Howard found a neglected walled garden near the historic Cowdray Ruins in England. A place where Henry VIII and Elizabeth I would have strolled once, thanks to Jan's vision and clever use of rusted iron structures, it's once again a formal garden fit for a king.

While searching for new premises for her award-winning company, Room in the Garden, Jan Howard came across a derelict walled garden adjacent to the grounds of the magnificent ruins of Cowdray, one of England's most important Tudor houses. The garden had once served as a vegetable garden, but after a fire devastated the original Cowdray house, it was abandoned. Jan was immediately inspired and agreed to a lease for the garden with the Cowdray Estate. With funds raised through her company she was able to breathe life back into this ancient garden.

Jan's design for the garden was to create a formal walled garden that reflected and enhanced its noble surroundings and was also a showcase for her collection of rusted iron plant supports, arches, pavilions, and gazebos. The end result? The perfect embodiment of a formal Tudor-style garden with a deliciously modern twist.

Gardens during the Tudor period were often formal, symmetrical, and enclosed by high walls or hedges. It's a treat to see authentic handmade brick walls nestle and enclose the Cowdray garden, creating a space that feels both private and protected. Large Tudor gardens also tended to mirror the alignment of the main house, creating a wonderful sense of continuity and harmony between architecture and outside space.

While this beautiful garden has all the familiar elements of a formal garden—roses, with lavender and box-edged borders, a raised central lawn, and numerous geometric beds—the stars of the show are undoubtedly Jan's rusted iron designs. The gazebos and dining pavilions with colorful liners create rooms around the garden, tranquil places to sit and the perfect space for outdoor entertaining. Some are left as beautiful sculptural structures, others colonized by scented climbing roses and clematis.

Pergolas and arches create elegant walkways and points of interest around the space; planted with roses, honeysuckle, clematis, or sweet peas, these delicate structures provide a sweetly scented and stunning addition to this garden. And plant supports of all forms and sizes not only provide focus for the eye, but also create rising formal shapes onto which Jan's flowers and foliage can cling throughout the changing seasons.

PREVIOUS PAGES, LEFT **Queen Elizabeth I famously declared** "I may not be a lion, but I am a lion's cub, and I have a lion's heart." How apposite, then, that the garden that received both her and her father, King Henry VIII, should proudly display a lion statue. PREVIOUS PAGES, RIGHT *The undeniable charm of an old English walled garden is brought to life with Jan Howard's rusted iron structures and a classical water feature.* RIGHT **A hexagonal gazebo, with a canvas roof, creates a room within a room, cleverly echoing the enclosed walled garden and creating a tranquil spot from which to enjoy the view.**

Relaxing spaces

There is an old Spanish proverb, "How beautiful it is to do nothing, and then to rest afterward." Relaxation is an essential part of our daily lives and yet one we find most difficult to organize. Our garden spaces, in particular, aren't always arranged in a way that makes it easy to enjoy a welcome break. That's where the laid-back charms of bric-a-brac furniture and kitsch collectibles really come into their element.

Architects have long understood that, when you're planning a space, you have to think about how it will work for the people using it. Aesthetics should start with broader ideas about how people are going to relax, eat, talk, and relate when they're milling around or sitting down. Creating a casual seating area outside needs just as much thought as a dining room or convivial kitchen—get it right and these special outdoor living areas enrich the pleasures of entertaining and transform everyday life, whether it's breakfast with birdsong, romantic meals at sunset, or cocktail parties with friends. The right configuration can invite conversation, encourage relaxation, and bring families closer together.

RIGHT *A retro classic, the stylish Acapulco chair was named after 1950s Hollywood's favorite beach destination, and epitomizes the decade of casual sophistication and chic celebrity.* OPPOSITE *From city center balconies to country verandas, we all want a relaxing outdoor space of our own; a place where we can entertain alfresco, take a catnap in the sun, or simply enjoy the view. It's life lived at a slower pace and the perfect backdrop for gardenalia.*

Vintage chairs and benches are the perfect accompaniment to a relaxed garden space. Life outside can be tough on furniture, so it's important not to be too precious about what you place in the garden—using secondhand pieces gives you permission to relax about the odd mark. The well-worn upholstery on an old chaise longue or the distressed paint on a Lloyd Loom armchair looks at home when it is placed against a natural backdrop. And, because it was designed to be used inside, when flea-market furniture is placed outside it provides an important link between home and garden, a place to unwind after work and enjoy being outside without feeling too far from the comfort of indoors.

Relaxing under cover—whether it's an overgrown pergola or a quirky entertaining shed—combines the best of domestic life, bringing the outdoors in and the indoors out. From country verandas to cool canopies, these fresh airy rooms create an easygoing space where we can cook and eat alfresco, take a nap in the sun, or enjoy the view sheltered from the weather but open to the elements.

Vintage gardenalia and secondhand pieces create the perfect mood for outdoor entertaining. School benches and industrial worktables provide instant seating for large groups, while a pair of church pews or antique benches will comfortably accommodate an intimate gathering. A throw, plump pillows, and a well-worn

rug will soften any hard surfaces and add to the inside/out illusion. Create a cheerful, summery feel with mismatched wooden chairs painted in ice-cream pastels or off-whites, kitsch florals, and vintage bunting. Fill vintage pitchers and pails with bright blooms and foliage. Opt for a retro look with salvaged office chairs, aluminum tables, and 1960s fabric prints, or create vacation chic with bentwood café chairs, wirework benches, and striped fabrics. For a pared-down, recycled look, team distressed wooden benches and chairs with neutral fabrics—sackcloth, calico, unbleached cotton, or linen; decorations made from raw materials and objets trouvés, such as candles, moss, river rocks, and driftwood, complete the look.

OPPOSITE *A pillow-filled, plump daybed beckons you invitingly to a quiet, secluded spot in a pretty courtyard garden. It would be hard to resist a quick nap on such a comfortable seat, softened with bolsters and a vintage mattress. ABOVE LEFT An icon of 1960s decor, rattan hanging chairs can be supported from a sturdy beam or a self-supporting steel frame. Original versions are collectors' items but modern repros are easy to source thanks to a revival in retro interiors. ABOVE RIGHT A vintage parasol creates a shaded, romantic corner in this small courtyard garden. An antique scrubbed pine table, café chair, and weathered wooden bench complete the look.*

Entertaining

When it comes to dining en masse, salvaged furniture creates inexpensive, large-scale seating in a hurry. Village hall trestles, pool tables, or antique cast-iron fencing topped with glass—almost any flat surface can be repurposed into a welcoming dining table. For large numbers of people, look toward public or institutional furniture—canteen tables, refectory benches, hospital gurneys, and industrial work surfaces. Architectural sections of wood—large doors, cupboards, floorboards, shutters, and paneling—also transform into dining tabletops on a grand scale.

Create a casual, knee-height table surface with a reclaimed railway trolley, wooden palette, or a vintage door on blocks. Large wooden cable drums and office coffee tables look quirky dragged out of context and into the stress-free surroundings of a garden. Glass-topped bird tables, stools, washstands, blanket boxes, sewing tables, shoe racks, butcher's blocks, and upturned crates all make quirky occasional tables for guests to place their glasses or plates. To add to the atmosphere, ceramic sinks, wheelbarrows, old coppers, oil drums, and laundry tubs filled with ice make instant drinks coolers, while old glass bottles, jars, and decorative cans make charming and inexpensive flower or candleholders.

When you are creating your outdoor dining space, give a thought to protecting your guests from the elements. A simple recycled tarpaulin or sail strung between the trees provides instant makeshift cover from sun and light showers or, for something more substantial, consider an antique gazebo or vintage canvas sun shelter. An old summerhouse or tool shed can easily be converted into an outdoor dining room, ensuring the weather won't ever spoil your fun. An overgrown trellis, arch, or gazebo will also provide a

PREVIOUS PAGES, LEFT **A summer shed is perfect for lazy afternoons and quiet catnaps. Distressed wooden furniture blends with the weather-beaten clapboard, lovingly accessorized with prints, lamps, and pillows in fresh ticking.** PREVIOUS PAGES, RIGHT **A barn fit for a manorial feast. Long wooden benches and** a generous refectory table create ample seating, topped off with an elegant handmade take on a gothic chandelier. RIGHT **Cheery bunting, floral tablecloths, and mismatched chairs have become shorthand for village fair chic and communal country entertaining. The look translates to any size garden.**

degree of protection—keeping the worst excesses of the midday sun from your guests. So many garden spaces focus on what's at ground level—the joy of creating a covered dining space or relaxing area is that you can build a structure that takes the eye upward and outward, making the space feel more expansive and exciting.

The biggest challenge with outdoor entertaining is keeping guests cozy when the evening draws in—providing plenty of natural wool blankets, throws, thrift shop pillows, and bolsters will keep guests toasty and warm and more inclined to linger. Vintage lanterns and flares will add spots of warmth, but for a real blast of heat use an old wood-burning chiminea or fire pit.

For maximum visual effect, think about where you are going to set the stage for your alfresco meal. It's tempting to plonk your table and chairs in the middle of the lawn but think of other spaces that might work better. A hidden corner of the garden or a meal among an orchard will create an intimate dining space—the plants and trees acting as walls and ceiling, perfect for hanging lanterns and tealights to brighten the dusk.

Push the chairs and tables right next to the house and rig up a canopy, and you create a street café vibe and have the added advantage of being close to the kitchen. The back wall of the house also makes the perfect backdrop for decoration, whether it's fairy lights or a fabric screen. Or, if you're lucky enough to have a large garden, create a dining space at the farthest point from the house. Part of the adventure of the evening will be picking your way down the garden path and eating a meal under the stars.

OPPOSITE *Sheltering under a wooden canopy, a diverse family of old church pews, lattice-work chairs, and a kitchen table creates a welcoming, weather-resistant dining area.* LEFT *Taking their chances alfresco, rusted café chairs gather around an old railroad trolley to make a charmingly impromptu evening picnic spot.*

Lighting

Lighting is one of the most underused elements of the garden and yet has the potential to add real drama and ambience to any outside space. Whether you want an outdoor chandelier or tiny tealights, antique lighting and recycled objects only add to the effect. The choices are dizzying. From storms lanterns to barn lights, fishing lamps to railway lanterns—lights that had an original purpose in an industrial or agricultural setting make a rustic addition to any garden, while spectacular indoor lighting—chandeliers, wall sconces, and candelabras—creates real glamour in an outdoor setting.

From Victorian street lamps to jam jar tealights, the size and scale of your lighting can be adapted to suit your space and budget. Experiment with different sources of lighting. A combination of vintage lights and recycled candle holders will create real sparkle and help to highlight key areas or plants around your garden. Make a large outside space feel cozy and intimate by adding clusters of lanterns or candle holders—group them in corners or on flat surfaces to create low pools of light. Well-worn chandeliers create a fabulous atmosphere of faded grandeur. Group three or more together for a truly sumptuous effect.

Use pierced tin cans or Moroccan-style lanterns to create patterns of light, and make the most of any reflective surfaces such as mirrors and water to bounce candlelight back and forth, perfect for adding that extra glow. Tealights provide dots of light or "runways" to guide your attention toward a focal point. Clustered in large groups they create pools of magical, twinkling light.

You can also use vintage and secondhand lighting on a more day-to-day practical basis. From the elegant simplicity of wall-mounted fishing lamps to the grand statement of a reclaimed street lamp, everyday outdoor lighting can be as inventive and original as you dare. Just make sure you get a qualified electrician to rewire any old-fashioned preregulation lights, especially for use outdoors.

ABOVE **Multiple vintage chandeliers create an opulent cluster of lights above this simple dining area and will provide a gentle, ambient glow well into the evening.**

Lamps and lanterns

- Lanterns and storm lights are ideal for wall mounting, providing background interest and portable illumination when needed.
- Pierced light-holders and Moroccan lanterns can make dazzling centerpieces for an outdoor dining table.
- Place tealights or small beeswax candles in terra-cotta pots for instant rustic decorations.

Home Comforts

When interior designer Bunny Williams tackles a garden, interesting things happen. Ideas about comfort and functionality suddenly begin to matter in a space usually reserved for plants. The results speak for themselves.

LEFT *This lush private courtyard is more like a living room, complete with open fire and relaxing vintage furniture.*
RIGHT **Playing with light.** *Sandy instinctively understands the importance of outdoor sparkle, cleverly laying different forms of lighting and candles to create a rich, welcoming atmosphere.*
OVERLEAF, LEFT *A vine- and flower-festooned garden room, created from huge salvaged windows, strikes the perfect note of faded glamour.*
OVERLEAF, ABOVE RIGHT **An** *outdoor kitchen sink with a fantastic reclaimed backsplash and curtained storage is perfect for impromptu outdoor meals.*
OVERLEAF, BELOW RIGHT *With such devilishly good detail, every tiny accessory adds to the vintage vibe. A milk bottle rack makes a charming centerpiece for an informal lunch.*

California Dreaming

California—a place renowned for its warm welcomes, endless sunshine, and laid-back charms—is the perfect place for leading designer Sandy Koepke to showcase her own distinctive style of garden decoration.

Ask Sandy Koepke about her unique style and there's only one word that fits the bill—"relaxed." "Not just a look, it's a feeling," she laughs. "I always say that to clients! It's not how it looks, it's how it feels." With someone who is as comfortable outside as in, there's always something going on in the garden, whether it's cooking with friends, potlucks, house guests, or playing with the dogs.

Sandy works hard, but her home is a sanctuary. In her courtyard the birds flit around, hummingbirds make tiny nests; there's a feeling of serenity and peacefulness. Bird feeders and little bubbler fountains are hidden away so the sound is subliminal and subtle. "I think I design the way I cook," she muses. "I'm rather free-form with great ingredients, adding a little imagination and fun. I'm not so good at following a recipe or a rule."

Vintage furniture and salvage treasures blend seamlessly into her philosophy. "I just love it. Love the patina and a little rust and a little silver plate or mirror gone bad. Worn stone, old pots, aged concrete. Nothing too perfect." Her experience has shown her that older, seasoned pieces integrate better into the garden and then, with age and weather, they just get better.

But well-worn unique one-off pieces can't just be picked off the shelf. Ditching showrooms in favor of flea markets, *brocantes*, estate sales, small one-owner shops, and thrift stores, it seems she leaves few sources of salvage unturned.

"I once picked up a wonderful neon sign by a dumpster that said 'California's Finest.' It looked great in an outdoor kitchen." On another occasion she rescued huge iron and glass windows from the estate sale of a movie set designer to re-create the feeling of an abandoned greenhouse. Sandy is also keen to use natural or recycled materials—stone, concrete, raw iron that rusts, copper sinks, unlacquered brass taps, old lanterns rewired. It's salvage used with a playful eye for drama and impact.

It helps that California has the perfect climate for living and entertaining outdoors. "People are more relaxed outdoors," she explains. "It's just a different atmosphere out here, particularly at night. I try to use layers of lighting—lanterns, strings of lights, old fixtures converted to low voltage, lots of candles—so there is a bit of romance. I try to make outdoor rooms beautiful and livable." And, judging by her results, she does exactly that.

Containers reclaimed

Outside space is a scarce commodity. For balconies, backyards, and small gardens, planting in vintage pots and containers is one of the best ways to get green-fingered. Containers also work well in large gardens and are an effective way to soften hard landscaping and bring seasonal richness to the front door.

For the time-pressed gardener, containers are a sneaky way of ringing the changes without much effort—a pot full of seasonal bulbs or spring blossom is like a well-chosen accessory, perfect for adding extra sparkle to an otherwise plain backdrop. Whether it's seasonal blooms or pots of potatoes, there's no quicker way to transform a stark flight of steps or a dull concrete terrace. It's also good to know that you don't have to be a seasoned expert to make a success of container gardening. Almost anything will grow—herbs, salad, vegetables, flowers, shrubs, soft fruit, even trees—as long as you provide the magic four ingredients: good drainage, light, water, and food.

RIGHT *Before the advent of washing machines, every household would have relied on its metal laundry tubs. Now obsolete, they serve an infinitely more relaxing purpose as pretty containers, bringing washes of color to any outside space.* OPPOSITE *Reclaimed metal containers come in many different guises. Rain barrels, florists' buckets, mixing bowls, baskets, cake pans, zinc trays, and many other types of metal pot create a richly textured backdoor display.*

As long as you can create some kind of drainage, and there's enough depth for growing medium, your choices are limitless. Chimney pots make fine, upstanding floral containers and work especially well in formal pairs. Ceramic basins and stone troughs create robust and practical planters for bulbs and succulents. Wire sconces filled with terra-cotta pots and vivid blooms add instant zing to a patio, while champagne boxes and zinc planters make cheerful window boxes or work well fastened to railings. Even the smallest container can be used inventively—decorative food cans and vintage tins make fantastic herb gardens. Buckets, oil drums, wicker baskets, cast-iron bathtubs, laundry tubs, wooden drawers—reclaimed containers can be found for no or little money.

When it comes to arranging your reclaimed containers, there's always safety in numbers. Small objects by themselves can get lost in a garden; group collections of similar containers in purposeful displays to create maximum effect. Small pieces of gardenalia, such as containers, also look better grouped by material or color. Stack terra-cotta pots vertically on a ladder or flight of steps, for example, or line them up on a shelf for a cohesive look. If they are placed against a contrasting background, even better.

Be inventive. It's always arresting to have something ugly or funny in a garden. To stop the too-perfect "showroom effect," find a container that's tattered, humorous, or just plain weird to create a conversation piece. A suitcase planted up with lavender, an old wine crate stuffed with herbs, an unwanted blanket box for cultivating tomatoes—anything as long as it's unique. Large containers look best against a plain backdrop. It's just like framing a picture—the simpler the background the better. An ivy-covered wall, a wooden fence, or hedge is perfect. If you've splashed out on an expensive container, display it in isolation. Don't clutter it with smaller pieces.

LEFT *An ancient, weather-beaten cart makes an arresting container for a glorious display of flowers. Agricultural sales and auctions often sell off redundant farming equipment, much of which transfers beautifully to a smaller setting.* OPPOSITE *An old flight of wooden stairs gets a surprising makeover as a plant theater for a riot of pink hyacinths. Despite their size, many pieces of architectural salvage like this cost very little as they can be difficult to refit into new houses or refurbishments.*

RIGHT *A glorious gaggle of mismatched containers, from terra-cotta bread bins to stone troughs, glazed plant pots to zinc feeders. Despite their differences the simple planting helps to corral this rowdy bunch into a well-behaved group.*

If you are planning a formal garden, stick to even numbers for small containers, such as a pair of urns. Rows or avenues of pots create a definite boundary wherever you use them and are excellent for delineating areas of lawn from pathways, or highlighting the edges of borders. Tall pots planted with seasonal bulbs are a fantastic way of bringing spots of color early in the year, while cascading groups of pots can create a bright corner or doorstep display. Formal gardens, which often rely heavily on evergreens, need bursts of color to bring them alive—colorful container plants, in a limited palette, are the ideal way to relieve the monotony without compromising the structure and simplicity of the space.

Informal schemes work better with odd numbers, especially threes and fives. And play with perspective. A really large container, such as a huge terra-cotta urn, will create a fantastic conversation piece and a focus for the rest of the garden. Splurge on lots of small pieces of garden salvage and crowd them together for a busy, eclectic feel; differently shaped Victorian clay pots, such as long toms, seed pans, strawberry planters, and bulb bowls, all offer a change from the usual plant pot shapes. Mismatched vintage teacups or teapots always add a whimsical note, while a riot of different-colored containers ensures an informal feel.

If you're working with a tiny space, such as a balcony, stick to a handful of colors and materials, otherwise the space can start to feel cramped. Reclaimed pots also don't have to be limited to ground level—they can work equally well attached to a wall, fence, wooden panel, or tree trunk. In a balcony garden, it's also important not to overcrowd. The empty spaces are just as important, to let air circulate and allow sunlight to reach as many leaves as possible.

OPPOSITE **Using containers at different heights adds a new dimension to your outside space. Here, the window sill, garden bench, and ground-floor level were all equally utilized as surfaces for terra-cotta pots and pretty zinc planters.** ABOVE RIGHT **Breathing new life into old objects, this resourceful gardener transformed unwanted** **agricultural feeders into striking wall planters filled with summer blooms.** RIGHT **Simple yet effective, this sparing collection of metal buckets and wooden half-barrels makes an elegant display of ivy and bedding plants. These spring flowers can be replaced with midseason blooms without too much disruption.**

Color Contained

Writer, cook, broadcaster, florist,
gardener, and teacher—Sarah Raven
is one of life's enviable polymaths. But
throughout her multiple talents runs a
common thread: whatever you do in life,
do it with color, boldness, and gusto.

Sarah Raven wrote, "A florist is like being a gardener. As you make a bunch of flowers, you collect colors, shapes, and textures together as you do in planting a garden, but you are making something that is a foot or two across, rather than several yards. It is an intensified version of the same process, yet liberating and free . . . it encourages you to be brave, to go for it, no holds barred."

It's perhaps no surprise that, with such a knack for creating bursts of color, Sarah is also a whiz at container gardening. With a florist's eye, she implicitly understands the power of plants to make a statement and this, combined with her love of strong and passionate colors, has helped to create one of Britain's most bright and dazzling garden spaces, at Perch Hill Farm in Sussex.

For Sarah, containers provide a pivotal role, adding extra layers of different shapes and architecture. Without them, she insists, the garden would look naked. But, as any gardener knows, there's an art to creating color in such a confined space, so what is her potted guide to reclaimed containers? One of Sarah's favorite tricks is to use tight rows or avenues of terra-cotta pots placed neatly on the edges of lawns or paths. Planted up with similar blooms, these containers give an instant sense of boundary and direction. And, in hidden corners, she plays with proportion, using one large pot as an attention-grabbing statement.

Pots must also harmonize with their surroundings. At Perch Hill Farm, for example, Sarah uses old galvanized troughs and barrels, weather-worn terra-cotta pots, and old oak planters—all modest materials that suit a rustic farm garden. When it comes to planting, bold is beautiful, but Sarah advises sticking to a narrow range or family of colors. Too many shades will compete for attention, rather than bring the garden together.

Terra-cotta works well time and time again. According to Sarah "the more weather-beaten the pot the better." You'll need good drainage, too—fill the bottom of the container with broken potsherds and stone—this will keep the roots from becoming waterlogged. The only exceptions are plants such as polyanthus, which prefer moist soil and work well planted up in a small serving bowl filled with multipurpose potting medium.

Once they're nicely bedded in, to keep the plants happy, pack them in tightly to deter weeds and keep the compost moist. And Sarah's top five plants for pots? *Acidanthera*, *Arctotis*, dahlias, Iceland poppies, and, of course, tulips by the bucket-load.

PREVIOUS PAGES, LEFT *A humble, square, unglazed planter provides the ideal foil for a display of irises.* PREVIOUS PAGES, RIGHT *Terra-cotta long toms always make a confident statement in a garden. Lined up like sentries, rows of uniform containers help to define edges and give direction to the space.* ABOVE *Metal rain barrels are a favorite choice for container gardeners. Here, Sarah used them almost as huge florists' buckets, displaying an* enormous "bouquet" of white tulips. RIGHT *Bold and brilliant, this hanging container creates an overflowing chandelier of flowers, gracefully adorning Sarah's sweet pea walkway.* ABOVE FAR RIGHT *An exquisite display of little crocuses made all the more perfect by their mellow terra-cotta bowl. These rustic containers can work well as pretty table centers.* BELOW FAR RIGHT *Wooden crates, silvered by the sun, always make effective containers.*

Colorful corners

Who says gardens have to be serious? Nothing beats the sheer undiluted pleasure of messing about with color, so why not use bright and bold vintage gardenalia to create a space that's packed full of personality and presence. Go on. Be bold.

As children, we innately understand the pleasure of bright color, mixing garish pinks, sky blues, and lemon yellows with aplomb. As grown-ups, we sometimes lose the confidence to be brave with our colors—it's all too easy to choose a limited palette or safe monochrome scheme for our gardens.

OPPOSITE *Small pieces of gardenalia look better grouped by material or color. Stack terra-cotta pots vertically, for example, or line them up on a shelf for a cohesive look. If they are placed against a bright background, even better.* RIGHT *The person who coined the phrase "Red and green should never been seen" didn't understand the power of complementary pairs. When green and red, blue and orange, or yellow and violet are placed next to each other, they make each other appear brighter.*

Forget safe. Have some fun. From colorful containers to vivid paint colors, vibrant fence panels to multicolored furniture, gardenalia is an instant way to add points of color throughout your outside space. Whether you want flashes of interest or a visual riot, it's helpful to think about the different layers of color you can add. Starting with the bones of the garden, many of the structures within an outdoor area come alive with color. From fence panels to brick walls, screens to metal railings, a quick lick of bright paint will add drama to vertical structures and create a useful backdrop for contrasting plants and containers. Even if space is limited, painting the wall of a shed or a trio of pots will lift a lifeless patio.

Think about what's going on underfoot. There's no reason you can't create a carpet of color by painting decking or concrete flooring with a hard-wearing finish. It's a fantastic way of brightening up a dull surface and a fail-safe way to make an area of hard landscaping feel more like a distinct room within a larger space. Certain building materials have natural color to start with—from rich red terra-cotta pavers to royal blue glazed tiles. Enjoy the process of using complementary opposites—red and green, blue and orange, and yellow and violet. Something magical happens when these colors are used in pairs—when placed next to each other complementary opposites appear brighter and more vivid.

If your garden beds are predominantly green, use painted obelisks and arches to provide visual spikes. During the long winter months, a garden can soon look desperate without any color—it's great to think that you don't have to rely on plants to do all the hard work.

Furniture and fabrics are an obvious source of color, especially when the season warms up. From the lollipop shades of retro office chairs to the Provençal charms of painted café tables, bright furniture will add an instant zing to your outside space. Striped deck chairs, windbreaks, and director's chairs lend a jolly seaside theme while rusty red terra-cotta pots, rich ocher walls, and dazzling blue accents create a rustic Italian feel.

Containers are a quick way to add a kaleidoscope of shades. Food packaging—especially cans—is often eye-catchingly bright with harlequin color and quirky writing. Large olive oil cans and catering-size tins make lively makeshift plant pots and look especially effective in large numbers. Bright watering cans, enamel buckets in bold colors, and painted terra-cotta pots work really well, too.

OPPOSITE, LEFT *Bold stripes of color always add a seaside note to your garden.* OPPOSITE, RIGHT *Blue is often associated with Provençal houses and gardens, perhaps because of its ubiquitous use on shutters, doors, and garden furniture. As a color, it also contrasts beautifully with the reds and oranges of handmade brick and terra-cotta, making it a natural choice for a cheery corner.* ABOVE LEFT *Red often works well in northern climes, where it provides a dazzling counterpoint to the lush greens of lawns, shrubs, and trees.* ABOVE RIGHT *This reclaimed red fence was ingeniously painted in different hues of red, replicating the color and form of the tree in the foreground. Small squares of bright yellow and chalky white also mimic the wildflowers, creating an abstract backdrop full of life and movement.*

171

Bright doesn't necessarily have to be chaotic, however. If you want to add color but in controlled bursts, restrict yourself to two contrasting hues. You can also use color to create a visual illusion; different colors create different effects. Warm colors—reds, oranges, and yellows—tend to attract the eye more readily than cooler colors, and make things appear closer than they are. You can use gardenalia in these "advancing" warms colors, therefore, to draw attention to parts of the garden or make a space feel smaller or more enclosed. Colors on the cooler side of the spectrum—blues, greens, and purples—create a receding effect, making something appear farther away or less noticeable.

To stop your outside space looking like a cacophony of color, follow the general rule that the brighter the gardenalia, the more simple the planting. Man-made and organic colors don't always sit well together—the natural brilliance of plant color can make man-made paints and finishes look cheap and garish. Or, conversely, a strikingly vivid paint color can leave even the blousiest of flowers looking pale and washed out.

ABOVE LEFT **Folk canal art, also known as "castles and roses," was traditionally used to decorate the outside of barges and all the equipment a boatman might need. Its naive but flamboyant style of decoration also suits many pieces of gardenalia such as watering cans and containers.** LEFT **Brutish oil drums suddenly become bright plant pots with a generous lick of paint.**

These work best planted with larger-than-life vegetables and shrubs, plants that can compete with the size and scale of the container. OPPOSITE **Food tins can be richly decorative. From vintage cookie to modern-day powdered milk containers, they easily convert to colorful containers. You can also reuse catering-size olive oil cans, and tomato soup, baked beans, and coffee cans.**

In the potting shed

Gardening is a timeless activity. Whether you are digging up weeds or planting seedlings, it's easy to imagine the green-fingered generations who've gone before. No wonder, then, that vintage tools and characterful pots should fit so easily into the modern-day potting shed.

There's pleasure in the simple beauty of vintage tools. From a favorite trowel to a trusty spade, these much-loved garden companions are central to our experience of gardening. They rely on us, too, to keep them dry and well maintained, ready for years of use. That's where a well-organized hut really comes into its own.

The potting shed is a special place. It's in here that the real alchemy of gardening goes on—the choosing of seed varieties, the endless agonizing over what to plant, and the hours lost engrossed in the simple pleasure of potting up. It's a practical space, but it's also a personal one. Tools, implements, and containers need to be organized to be useful, but they can also create gratifying displays in themselves. There's as much pleasure to be had from a tidy rack of spades as a pretty row of plants.

The shed is also a place for thinking and reminiscing. Using vintage tools and old-fashioned methods reminds us of childhoods spent in our parents' or grandparents' gardens—of homegrown vegetables, seasonal flowers, and ripening orchards. The attraction of gardenalia is more than just its usefulness or beauty. If we are honest with ourselves, gardenalia speaks to our nostalgic selves. We might be indulging in a bit of fantasy, but it's an effective escape from the hustle and bustle of modern life.

Vintage tools and garden collectibles are a joy to use. Anything that gets put to work in the garden needs to be well made and robust. And whether it's a sturdy fork or a tiny thumb pot, most practical gardenalia comes from an era when raw materials, craftsmanship, and attention to detail were second-to-none. Many of the vintage tools that we see today have survived because of their inherent build quality. It says a lot that even in our modern, high-tech age we're still deeply traditional when it comes to our

LEFT *Vintage tins, old pots, and well-loved tools lift garden tasks to a sublime new level and prove to be robust, faithful companions.* OPPOSITE *Little has changed from the early twentieth century in terms of the design and function of garden tools. And why should it? Many years of gardening experience have shown just how well suited vintage tools are to the challenge of twenty-first-century gardening.*

BELOW RIGHT **Every gardener needs a quiet corner to pot up plants and take a well-earned break. Here, a rustic stool makes a practical, unfussy choice for seating and, when not in use, doubles as a handy side table.** *RIGHT* **The odd flash of bright steel is the only giveaway separating the modern and antique tools on display. Hanging spades and forks on the wall is the ideal way to care for garden tools, keeping dampness and potential for damage at bay.** *OVERLEAF, LEFT* **Well loved and well cared for, these traditional tools will see years of service if they continue to be maintained so beautifully.** *OVERLEAF, RIGHT* **All manner of age-old gardenalia is on show in this country corner. From lanterns to sifters, dibbles to shears, each vintage tool is a little slice of garden history.**

potting sheds. Labor-saving devices and high-tech solutions simply can't complete with the well-worn charms of a vintage spade or weather-beaten cloche. Vintage tools have personalities, too—they don't suffer from the bland uniformity that often blights modern implements. There are some wonderful regional differences. Take the spade, for example, which can vary from a pointed, triangular shovel, to long-handled spades for agricultural use. In areas with heavy clay soils a treaded blade was common so you could put more pressure on the spade with your foot. Each one has its own distinct character and pleasure in use. Storage is always an issue in such a compact space. Salvaged and secondhand cupboards are a tough, practical option. It's important they can take the odd knock and bang, so industrial cupboards or school lockers are always a handsome choice.

Fruit crates, either stacked or on castors, make ideal storage for smaller items, while rows of terra-cotta pots can always double as storage when they're not being put to use in the garden. Bookcases and shoe racks work really well for storing pots, watering cans, and smaller items, but you can easily create shelving with salvaged planks and reclaimed bricks or upside-down terra-cotta pots as spacers. You can't have too many hooks and hangers either—redundant trowels and handforks make quirky pegs for hanging aprons or bags.

In terms of practicalities, most old hand tools are elegantly simple and easy to repair, provided you take your time. After a hard day's digging, here's what you should do to keep your vintage tools in tip-top condition:

Remove any residual soil and chemicals from the tool as both can cause corrosion. A gentle wipe will do, but if you need to rinse your tools make sure you dry them completely before hanging them up to prevent rust. Hang them up. This is so you can access your tools quickly but primarily because it keeps them off any damp surfaces and stops them from knocking into each other (which can blunt sharp edges and cause splinters). Keep your potting shed dry and regularly check tools for woodworm or rust. Keep any cutting surfaces sharp. Sharp tools are actually safer to use than blunt ones because you don't have to use as much force. Damaged tools are dangerous to use so quickly repair any breakages and keep wooden handles smooth and split free. All metal tools are prone to rust. Get rid of rust by rubbing it off with something abrasive like wet/dry paper or wire wool and then apply oil or wax. The best prevention, however, is frequent use so enjoy using your vintage tools as much as possible. If you ever needed an excuse to get out into the potting shed, there's one.

*ABOVE LEFT **A potting bench needs to be solid and scrubbable. Rough and ready reclaimed lumber is the ideal material, taking anything the gardener can throw at it.** LEFT **A vintage garden trug, one of the most pleasing and pretty pieces of gardenalia. The sheer breadth of shapes and varieties available makes them just the job** for everything from harvesting vegetables to gathering cut flowers, storing fruit to collecting eggs.** OPPOSITE **An experienced gardener could want for little in this vintage-packed greenhouse. From a battered armchair to elegant plant supports, rustic enamelware to balls of traditional twine, it's potting shed perfection.**

Liz Butterfield, the Engagement Gardener at Nunnington Hall, is unperturbed about having to be a resourceful gardener. In fact, she relishes the challenge; a "make-do-and-mend" philosophy sits comfortably with her own creative but deeply practical style of gardening. An enthusiastic collector of antiques, curios, and auction finds, Liz enjoys putting all manner of gardenalia to use in the cutting garden. From wine crates to seedling trays, old spades to reclaimed tiles, it's a space brimming with garden collectibles and salvage style. Even the shed itself was salvaged; rescued from an ignored corner of the estate, dragged across to the grounds by an army of willing volunteers, lovingly repainted and crammed with the vintage tools and accessories collected by Liz and previous gardeners over the years.

A handmade brick path winds its way among the vegetables, an old zinc trash can doubles up as a handy planter for zucchinis, and tiny terra-cotta thumb pots make dinky cane toppers around the beds. Plant markers are created from coppiced hazel sticks, cleverly sliced on an angle to reveal a perfect flat writing surface, while neat rows of old-fashioned rhubarb forcers add to the patchwork effect.

But make no mistake—nothing is purely for show. This is a working garden. The tools and pots may have all the delightful patina and inherent beauty that comes with decades of use, but they still have to earn their keep if they are to stay in use. Vintage wicker baskets are pressed into service when it's time to harvest the season's organic fruit and vegetables; cut flowers find their way into old zinc florists' buckets and galvanized pails; and terra-cotta pots shelter the new year's seedlings or make handy containers for stray pencils and plant labels.

OPPOSITE, ABOVE LEFT **Twine, old pots, slate plant markers, and a vintage radio—all the essentials.** *OPPOSITE, ABOVE RIGHT* **Zinc florists' buckets, baskets, and galvanized pails make the journey from flowerbed to main house, carrying seasonal flowers.** *OPPOSITE, BELOW LEFT* **Vintage wooden baskets, sifters, and crates make light work of many garden tasks. In the background** is an old estate roller.
OPPOSITE, BELOW RIGHT **Terra-cotta thumb pots, many proudly displaying their maker's marks, are stacked neatly away on an old painted wooden shelf.** *RIGHT* **There are few concessions to modernity in Liz's plot. Most of the tools and equipment are generations old. Even the wicker chair was a hand-me-down and offers a welcome resting place.**

Garden Treasure Trove

A beautiful sixteenth-century manor house sits quietly on the banks of the River Rye in North Yorkshire, England. Nunnington Hall and its gardens are now in the hands of the National Trust and every penny counts, even in the potting shed.

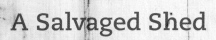

A Salvaged Shed

At the bottom of a garden, tucked behind an overgrown laurel, sits an unpromising potting shed. Created from reclaimed bricks and salvaged windows, this rickety old building looks like a brisk breeze might blow it over at any moment, but this is the author Sally Coulthard's treasured potting shed.

It's a potting shed created from scrap. And yet, despite its patched roof and wonky door, this is a cherished, deeply practical space. Cobbled together by the previous owner of our house, it's now my potting shed and a place I come to for all sorts of reasons: to plant up herbs, collect seeds, escape the incessant phone calls. I hide in here—cup of tea and cookie ration never far away—surrounded by some of my favorite old tools, watering cans, and tins.

Reclaimed York stone slabs provide a robust, sensible floor to cover the beaten earth. On a winter's day they're freezing underfoot, but come the spring, the stones seem to store up the sun's rays, providing ambient heat well after the sunshine's disappeared. It's a seasonal space but that doesn't matter—there's real excitement that comes from waiting for the warm weather to arrive so I can get back into my shed and start some serious potting.

Two old wooden racks sit propped against the back wall, rescued from a farmer friend about to consign them to the bonfire, and groaning under the weight of fruit crates, wicker baskets, pots, and watering cans. I need only one watering can but can't seem to resist picking up more along the way—seven at the last count and always room for one more. They've become a display as well as a resource—spouts pointing in the same direction like a trumpet fanfare.

My metal bench seat and old wooden table cost nothing. The former was a gift from my husband, who lovingly liberated it from a dumpster. The table was originally a school desk, donated by a friend who'd moved house with it one time too many and got fed up.

On the desk sits a long, wooden box. It's a handsome thing and once belonged to a vet who kept metal syringes in it, but it now makes a fine holder for seed packets. Next to it, another small wooden box, this time a vintage medicine cabinet now employed as a handy area for small bottles and jars. Dotted around are old tobacco and candy tins—contents long gone but perfect for storing collected seeds, envelopes, labels, and pieces of chalk.

Leaning against the walls of the shed are numerous vintage tools. I should hang them up, but I fear the shed wouldn't stand it, so I prop them guiltily on the floor and hope they don't mind. From antique hayforks to hoes and trowels, they make agreeable companions and still work beautifully around the garden. And in one corner, a pile of terra-cotta pots sits waiting to be used; tucked away, just in front, sits a cheerful gnome and a 1970s milk bottle rack—rusty, retro, and the perfect container for herb-filled terra-cotta pots.

PREVIOUS PAGES, LEFT *Salvaged windows, reclaimed bricks, and an old ledge and brace door create the bones of this rickety but romantic potting shed.* PREVIOUS PAGES, RIGHT *Necessity is the mother of invention; almost every element was begged, borrowed, and rescued from flea markets, dumpsters, and thrift stores.* RIGHT *A secondhand wooden rack is given a new lease on life as ample storage for wicker baskets, tools, and fruit crates.* OPPOSITE, ABOVE LEFT *Poppy seeds picked from a waste patch—with a little luck and a lot of patience they might add to next year's wildflower crop.* OPPOSITE, ABOVE RIGHT *A retro milk bottle holder makes a cutesy kitsch herb rack, tucked in a light corner of the shed.* OPPOSITE, BELOW LEFT *A 1960s stripy deck chair adds a welcome splash of color, hung on the wall like a piece of modern art.* OPPOSITE, BELOW RIGHT *Vintage candy, toffee, and tobacco tins make watertight storage for a multitude of gardening knickknacks.*

At work and play

Your garden is more than just a green space. It's also the perfect place for work and play. With the right furniture and fittings, your outdoor room can combine the best of vintage living with the pure pleasure of a life lived outdoors.

Whether you are hanging your laundry or tapping away on a laptop, many of life's chores turn into delights when you take them outside. We spend such a large proportion of our time indoors it's refreshing to get out into the garden and feel the sun on our backs. It's the same pleasure that comes from camping outdoors—tasks such as laundry, cooking, cleaning, and washing are infinitely more fun when they're done in makeshift surroundings. An old ceramic basin and a driftwood mirror create a rustic outdoor bathroom, a battered closet and wood-burning chiminea make an instant kitchen, or a vintage school desk and café chair form the basis of an outdoor office. Thankfully, much of the modern technology we rely on to help us is eminently portable—most of us only need a cell phone and a laptop—so we can feel connected even if we're hiding at the bottom of the garden. And, when the working day is over, there's no need to run indoors. All work and no play makes for a dull garden—thanks to lazy hammocks, swings, and vintage recliners, there are lots of ways to relax and enjoy your outside space.

LEFT *A traditional rope and box-frame garden swing is a timeless addition to a mellow orchard and a welcome antidote to modern plastic counterparts.*
OPPOSITE *Even workaday chores such as washing and drying can be lifted by the nostalgic unhurried pleasure of using traditional tools and old-fashioned kit.*

Play

There's no reason children should have all the fun. Whether it's a game of tennis or a garden swing, there are lots of ways you can bring antique games and collectibles into the garden to help you have fun. Vintage croquet sets, tennis nets, giant sized chessboards, horseshoes, target practice, skittles, garden dominoes, pétanque, or boules sets—there's a whole toy box of early and mid-twentieth-century collectible garden games to choose from. Not only do they provide a burst of fun, but they also make whimsical garden decorations when they're not being played with or are past their useful life.

If the kids feel left out, vintage or secondhand playhouses are a great way to fire their imagination. Modern plastic playhouses lack something of the Peter Pan charms of an old-fashioned Wendy house—look for traditional wooden examples, which can soon be brought back to life with a lick of paint and some bright curtains. If you're really handy, making a treehouse or den from salvaged lumber will give children freedom and independence and a place to escape to. As with all things you make or restore for children, you

need to be confident there aren't any safety issues. A few simple rules should keep your kids from harm: to stop fingers from being trapped, leave an inch gap along the door hinge or fit a piano hinge (which covers the entire gap); use magnetic catches to stop small children from locking themselves in; any upper or mezzanine floors more than 2 feet off the ground will need a rail; and keep all surfaces free from splinters and protruding screws or nails.

OPPOSITE *Space to learn, dream, and play. Children thrive on outdoor play and nothing expands the imagination like a gingerbread cottage at the end of the garden.* ABOVE LEFT *Playtime for adults can be just as fun. Here a game of tennis is umpired from a gorgeous* *vintage awning and spectators' chairs.* ABOVE RIGHT *This tremendous treehouse, neatly hidden among the leaves, makes a fantastic lookout. On the lawn below, a miniature Lloyd Loom chair, 1940s push-along dog, and wooden cart create a feeling of bygone childhoods.*

ABOVE *From painting landscapes to throwing pots or sewing quilts, there are few hobbies that can't be enjoyed from the happy surroundings of a shed filled with vintage treasures and hand-me-downs.* OPPOSITE *Nothing beats the natural light when you paint* en plein air *and this makeshift studio provides work surface and storage in one. A metal retro chair is ideal impromptu seating, softened with a 1960s-style cushion.*

Work

Imagine if your daily commute involved padding down the garden with your laptop and a cup of tea? More and more people are choosing not only to work from home, but also to work from the natural surroundings of their back garden. And whether it's a vintage shed or "shoffice" or a simple workbench under the trees, life couldn't get more productive and pleasurable at the same time. Often our best ideas come when we're outdoors, so why not get out into the fresh air and use vintage gardenalia and flea-market finds to create relaxed, practical working surroundings?

The popularity of the garden work space is justly deserved. Not only does it mean you can cut down on your travel time, but it also provides a cost-effective alternative to building an extension to your house. In a matter of days you can transform a humble shed into a state-of-the-art, all singing, all dancing office or studio. And all just a few steps from your back door.

From secondhand sheds to recycled office chairs, charming school desks to wooden benches, you can pick and choose your decor from the mountain of salvaged furniture that ends up in thrift shops, reclamation yards, and yard sales. Vintage shepherd's huts and gypsy wagons create glamorous, go-to-work sheds but there are other more unusual salvaged structures to choose from depending on your budget—from retro trailer tents to ex-army vehicles, antique revolving summer houses to upturned boat hulls; the only limit is your imagination. Mix and match the interior styling to create a characterful, creative work space—industrial chairs teamed with a rustic desk, retro task lighting with floral fabrics, metal storage boxes with wicker baskets. Don't restrict yourself to furniture and accessories primarily designed for offices. From chicken-wire egg baskets to metal picnic tables, battered armchairs to elegant chandeliers, the best vintage working spaces cherry-pick great design whatever form it comes in.

In fact, whatever the work, vintage accessories can turn a chore into a pleasure. When it comes to domestic jobs, antique clothes dryers, handmade wooden pegs, old-fashioned twine, laundry baskets, enamel buckets, vintage coal scuttles, galvanized garbage cans, wooden stepladders, and traditional brushes and pans are still up to the job. Many of these age-old accessories still work brilliantly around the home and garden, adding a touch of nostalgia and commonsense simplicity to workaday tasks such as laundry.

The Shepherd's Hut

On an 1856 map of Sally Coulthard's Yorkshire farm you can very clearly see the orchard; rows of apple and damson trees neatly planted and ready to provide the farmer and his wife with an abundant crop. Over 150 years later, the orchard is still here, as fruitful and mellow as it's always been.

PREVIOUS PAGES, LEFT *Vintage leather toddler boots, retro pint-sized gardening tools, and tin toys make a pretty vignette on this Provençal blue children's chair.* PREVIOUS PAGES, RIGHT *A child-sized shepherd's hut, made using age-old techniques and materials, is a timeless focal point for an apple-picking picnic.* RIGHT *An old flight of attic steps, borrowed from the farmhouse, forms a sturdy ladder for reaching the highest branches, while wicker and straw baskets—picked up from French brocantes—await their bounty below.* OPPOSITE, LEFT *A makeshift chandelier of vintage teacups, enamel lanterns, and glass candle holders creates a twinkling display as evening falls.* OPPOSITE, RIGHT *An ancient wine crate from the nearby city of York makes a handy perch to sit and enjoy a refreshing glass of soda. Cookies are safely stowed away from prying hens in an old salt tin.*

As a family, the orchard is one of our favorite spaces. Cool in the summer, bountiful in the fall—we rely on its seasonal produce, not only for the occasional fruit pie but also as a source of traditionally pressed apple juice and cider. The hens love it, too, greedily pecking at any windfall we're too slow to gather in time.

There's nothing better than enjoying your own produce, but there's a large amount of graft to be done before we can sit and sip. If we're to get it done before the season's over, the whole family needs to be pressed into picking—and that includes our two small daughters Madeleine and Isabella. Easier said than done.

To sweeten the deal, I made the girls a miniature shepherd's hut, a space they could rest and relax in between the hard work. Inspired by the full-sized versions, it's gardenalia on a grand scale and yet small enough not to dominate the outside space. With vintage iron wheels and old-fashioned tongue-and-groove timber cladding, it makes a playful space for the kids without spoiling the view. It's also a focal point for the grown-ups—providing a splash of color during the long, gray months and a nostalgic conversatin piece.

To keep things traditional, I wanted a canvas roof, but one that could withstand the elements. Victorian railway carriages used cotton canvas, glued and painted. After a few sticky experiments, and some useful tips from railway enthusiasts, the technique was perfected and created a watertight but vintage-looking roof. It's already been three different colors. That's not any fault of the children, but rather a quirk of my character. Never satisfied and ever curious, I can't help but experiment with historic shades. But that's the beauty of wood, forgiving of a contrary owner.

Keen to put their own stamp on it, the girls have been quick to personalize the hut. An old blanket box stores throws and pillows, ready for a teddy bear picnic, while a set of brightly painted children's chairs and an old miniature armchair create instant seating. Baskets, boxes, and vintage tins make cheap and cheerful storage, while an old length of ticking makes an excellent awning when it threatens to shower. The girls love it. The only problem is persuading them to stop playing in the hut and come and help mom and dad collect the apples.

The Gardener's Rest

Imagine a space that's so much more than a shed. Take all the tools at a gardener's disposal and mix them with quirky decorations and secondhand furniture. The result? The perfect garden retreat for work, rest, and play.

198

PREVIOUS PAGES, LEFT *A delicate antique table creates subtle support for this arrangement of plants in vintage terra-cotta pots.*
PREVIOUS PAGES, RIGHT *Always have something unusual or amusing in your garden space to stop the too-perfect "showroom effect." Something eye-catching, humorous or oversized—such as a giant letter or two—creates a conversation piece.* ABOVE *Plain whitewashed wood creates a blank canvas on which to display rows and clusters of garden collectibles.* OPPOSITE, LEFT *Blurring the boundary between outside and in, this garden retreat uses garden ornaments to create a cozy, welcoming atmosphere.* OPPOSITE, RIGHT *Simple, natural materials sing when placed side by side. Hessian, terra-cotta, lumber, and rusted metals create balance and harmony in this artful arrangement.*

Some people eat, sleep, and breathe gardening. And what better way to indulge that passion than create an outdoor room with almost everything a gardener's heart could desire? This simple whitewashed barn has been transformed into a horticultural haven with the help of gardenalia. Against the plain white clapperboard walls, simple metal shelves hold a bountiful array of old tools, vintage bird boxes, magazines, botanical prints, and other flea-market treasures. Old wicker baskets, shears, and working hand tools also find their way onto the wall, cleverly hung out of harm's way on makeshift hooks to create an eye-catching display.

A single bed makes a cozy corner, perfect for a midafternoon nap between garden chores and lit by an ingenious lantern on an old industrial pulley. Simple linens and sackcloth bring softness to

the space, without compromising the neutral color scheme. At the end of the bed is a bright blue secondhand set of shelves—perfect for odds and ends and the only splash of contrasting color in this sophisticated but earthy color palette. A potting table, created from handmade bricks and a sturdy work surface, houses a fine collection of weather-beaten terra-cotta pots and vintage wooden crates. Above the potting table, more impromptu shelving, this time carrying old-fashioned bell cloches, wine bottles, and a zinc bucket.

In fact, containers come in all shapes and sizes in this gardener's retreat, some with a practical purpose, others for sheer pleasure. A galvanized rain barrel and old milk churn both make generous containers for long-handled tools, spades, and brooms. Three clear glass bottles holding dahlias create a powerfully spartan flower

arrangement and terra-cotta long toms make ideal planters for indoor ferns and evergreens. The space is deeply practical and yet there's a whimsical hand at work here. An old wooden barrow makes a bygone container for lush plants while a small ornamental horse plays with perspective, making the room and its contents feel larger than life. Huge reclaimed letters spell the word "SOIL" across the back wall—an ingenious piece of wall sculpture and a tribute to the art of gardening.

Animal sanctuaries

From chic coops to busy bug boxes, driftwood bird tables to old-fashioned arks, whether you want to attract wildlife into your garden or give your chickens something to crow about, animal sanctuaries have never been so chic.

Insects and bees

While comfort and welfare must top the list when it comes to animal housing, there's still lots of room for vintage and handmade flair. Even our flying friends can have five-star accommodation. From bug houses to beehives, there are lots of ingenious ways you can bring insect life into your outside space. Wooden beehives come in different shapes and sizes, thanks to regional and historical variations. From the cottage garden appeal of the WBC hive (the classic beehive shape with the pointed roof that takes its name from its English designer William Broughton Carr) to the flat-topped French Dedant beehive, traditional wooden hives add instant vintage honey-jar appeal to a garden and provide a practical, healthy space for your colony. Basket skeps, although pretty to look at, aren't a good option for either bee or keeper, as the only way to harvest the honey is to destroy the colony.

Solitary bees, which act as important pollinators, need a different place to stay. They make their nests in hollow twigs and reeds, or holes in wood, so it's easy to make your own bee box from untreated wood, old flower stems, short logs, bamboo canes, or redundant bird houses. Either drill holes into a solid chunk of wood or bundle together short lengths of hollow stems or canes and secure with string or a wooden frame. These dinky homes also provide snug, safe bedrooms for other beneficial insects such as spiders, ladybugs, and lacewings. Just remember to put your bug box somewhere warm, dry, and out of the wind and rain, or your guests might not make it through the winter. Make more than one box, and place them at different heights around the garden, as different bugs hibernate at different levels.

OPPOSITE *A traditional WBC slatted beehive with its houselike pointed roof makes an architectural focal point among dense planting. Beehive-shaped compost bins also work well, especially if the challenge of beekeeping isn't appealing.*

LEFT *A quirky bug hotel has several different suites for picky guests. Garden-friendly insects take up residence, making nests in between the twigs and branches.*

LEFT Dovecotes were a common sight across Europe between the sixteenth and nineteenth centuries, so if you want to add a touch of history, traditional dove and pigeon houses lend a formal air to any garden. They come in a variety of shapes, from the gingerbread charms of triangular wall-mounted dovecotes to the stately glamour of rectangular and octagonal freestanding dovecotes.

Boxes and feeders

- You can add a note of whimsy, humor, folk art, homespun charm, or architectural flair with a homemade or vintage bird house.
- An old muffin pan loaded with tasty treats looks charming and will attract grateful flocks.
- A hole and a perch are all that is needed to transform anything into a cozy home—even an old straw hat hung on a sheltered wall.

Birds

Our feathered friends need all the help they can get. Vintage bird boxes and handcrafted huts are an ideal way to encourage wild birds into your garden and will also provide spots of color and visual interest at different heights all year round.

The design of bird boxes has changed little over the last two hundred years, so secondhand and collectible examples will work as effectively as the day they were made. The construction of a simple bird box is also so straightforward that it's easy to create one from salvaged timber or driftwood. All bird boxes need to be secure and weatherproof, and out of reach of potential predators, but different birds need different houses. The size of the hole at the front of the house will determine what nests there, and open-fronted bird boxes will make cozy homes for robins, wrens, and blackbirds. In terms of siting your bird box, make sure it's at least 5 feet from the ground.

Fix it to a wall or tree, in a quiet corner of your yard. The entrance hole should face anywhere between north and east—this protects the inhabitants from overheating in summer and the worst of the weather in winter. Most wild birds are territorial, too (apart from sparrows, who will happily nest in a community), so don't place lots of bird boxes next to one another.

And don't forget to provide an ample supply of food. Vintage bird feeders have become quite collectible—from heart-shaped feeders designed to hold an apple to gazebo-shaped wirework peanut holders, they not only provide a welcome meal for the birds but also add a touch of farm chic to your plot. Amost any salvaged receptacle can be transformed into a feeder if placed at a safe height. From vintage teacups to hubcaps, if you hang it from a tree or prop it on a stand, wild birds will find it and feed.

ABOVE **It's a dog's life. A vintage wooden dog kennel makes a cozy, rustic corner for a fortunate pooch.** *OPPOSITE* **Three Shaker-style coops create a chicken commune in this garden. The basic design of coops is similar— perch, nesting box, roof—so you can inject some creativity customizing a henhouse's appearance with poultry-friendly paints, accessories, and quirks.**

Pets and chickens

Poultry can be pretty picky. From fancy chicken coops to floating duck houses, there's a delightful range of traditional and vintage-style housing on offer. On a basic level, poultry need somewhere warm, dry, and secure. Chickens also need a perch to sleep on and nesting boxes to lay in. Beyond these simple requirements, it's more about the owner than the bird, but there's no reason you can't create something architectural, whimsical, striking, or rustic to add a flourish to your garden. From Shaker-style houses to converted tool sheds, old dog kennels to mock-villages, practical and pretty chicken huts aren't mutually exclusive. You can find shepherd's huts for hens, chicken caravans, and water-side duck pavilions on the

Internet, and the fun doesn't have to stop there. Vintage feeders, old water troughs, and zinc buckets all add to the rustic effect and help keep your henhouse clean and smart. Farm sales and agricultural auctions are a great place to find coops, runs, and duck houses, especially if you want housing on a commercial scale.

Man's best friend can also get in on the act. They don't come up very often, but occasionally antique dog kennels and wrought-iron dog enclosures find their way into auctions and salvage yards. Usually commissioned by wealthy owners these relics—from stone dog kennels to wooden traveling boxes—are often very grand and make smart housing for modern pooches. They don't come cheap,

however. At recent Christie's auctions in London a late nineteenth-century Victorian oak dog kennel, with a gothic-style arched door, an antique French painted wood and gesso dog kennel, made to resemble a stately home, and a small Victorian fruitwood kennel all sold for the price of a small car. Early and mid-twentieth-century examples, however, are easier and cheaper to source and repair if necessary. Most are softwood, and can be prone to rot or woodworm, so check your kennel is safe and comfortable for its new occupant. If in doubt, a traditional-style kit kennel is a good option and can be easily decorated with heritage paint colors for an authentic vintage feel.

When she was a six-year-old girl, Tiffany Kirchner Dixon's parents escaped the hustle and bustle of California and moved to the Pacific Northwest to buy a farm. From an early age, she was surrounded by fruit trees, vast fields, and farm animals. Fresh milk from the cows, vegetables from the garden, and working the land were all part of daily life. That kind of upbringing is hard to shake. When she was twelve, Tiffany's father's job took the family overseas to Hong Kong, a far cry from the bucolic bliss of farm life. Every summer, they returned to the farm and tried to reclaim what the last eleven months had deprived them of.

Certain that she would become a farmer herself, as an adult Tiffany finally settled upon a gentleman's farm big enough to house a few horses, her beloved mini burros, pet sheep Margaret, and over forty rare breed chickens. With farming in the blood, along with an inherited passion for all things vintage, it seems inevitable that Tiffany would go on to combine these two passions into a trademark style. As a child, her house was always filled with family heirlooms and characterful pieces, so it's no surprise that Tiffany picks up her favorite finds in thrift stores, flea markets, and antique shops. Drawn to things out of the ordinary, she's always ready to repurpose quirky treasures into conversation pieces for the farm.

For the chickens, Tiffany set to work personalizing a basic wooden coop with salvaged materials. Secondhand windows allow light to stream into the coop and make a perfect hatch to keep the chickens safe at night. An old porch door from an early 1900s house, stripped of its screen and replaced with chicken wire, creates an ideal partition to divide the hens from the food storage.

Neighborhood yard sales are a rich seam for Tiffany's keen-eyed searches and the place she discovered the antique barn ladder that now works as a perch for the hens to reach their nest boxes and roost on at night. Like a magpie, Tiffany always finds herself drawn to galvanized metal, a vintage farm must-have. Not only is the metal charming, but it's functional, too, and she uses galvanized buckets with locking lids to store feed for the animals. A vintage garbage trolley holds the shiny buckets and makes it easy for her to wheel around the heavy containers. An antique sifter hangs in the coop as a flower pot, and an age-worn armchair allows Tiffany to take a well-earned break after cleaning the coop. She doesn't mind that the stuffing is falling out, it only adds to the charm, and her handmade feed sack pillow adds extra comfort.

The Fancy Farmgirl

Imagine a farmer who also has a sensational eye for gardenalia. In Seattle, photographer and Fancy Farmgirl blogger Tiffany Kirchner Dixon creates extraordinary chicken coops from quirky collectibles and junkyard materials.

PREVIOUS PAGES, LEFT **A** *reclaimed porch door, infilled with chicken wire, makes an ideal boundary between birds and feed bins.* PREVIOUS PAGES, RIGHT *Admiring the view, one of Tiffany's four dozen fancy foul in her shabby-chic chicken coop.* RIGHT **A** *yard-sale barn ladder makes a fitting perch and point of access for chickens looking to nest. Once they've laid, Tiffany collects the eggs in one of her many flea-market buckets or farm-sale wire baskets.* OPPOSITE, ABOVE LEFT **Sharing** *the hutch with the hens, a well-loved rabbit doorstop keeps watch, propping open the screen door for cleaning and egg collection.* OPPOSITE, ABOVE RIGHT **A** *well-worn armchair is the perfect resting spot, adding a hint of faded grandeur to this opulent coop. A homemade feed sack pillow finishes the look.* OPPOSITE, BELOW LEFT *Galvanized bins store feed for hungry chickens. A vintage garbage trolley makes moving these heavy bins just that little bit easier.* OPPOSITE, BELOW RIGHT *Numbers and lettering always add character and visual surprise to a space. A large number six works brilliantly here, creating echoes of a domestic front door.*

THE PRACTICALITIES

While there's an almost infinite variety of gardenalia on offer, the same practical rules apply when it comes to sourcing and securing it. Most gardenalia is inexpensive and freely available, but for those rarer, more expensive pieces it pays to know what you should be looking for and how to keep it safe.

Establishing provenance

Provenance is basically the history of the ownership of an object. It matters in the antique gardenalia world for two reasons:

If an object has an exciting or interesting provenance it can add hugely to its value. People who buy antique and vintage items value not only the item itself but also its story—they want to know who owned it, where it came from, what kind of life it has had so far. Objects don't just have an intrinsic value—it's the meaning we attach to them that makes them important and collectible. Take an eighteenth-century garden statue, for example. One without provenance has a certain amount of value—we recognize that the materials and labor to create it are worth something. But add an exciting provenance such as a celebrity owner or a famous sculptor and the value skyrockets.

Sadly, provenance is also important for a more sinister reason. The antique trade has a murky side—thefts and fakes are commonplace. Establishing provenance is an important tool in the fight against illegally obtained and phony antiques.

Establishing provenance sometimes requires a bit of persistence. Lots of different clues can piece together to create a complete picture—receipts, gallery documents, auction catalogs, ownership records and wills, magazine or newspaper articles, letters of authentication from experts, original factory catalogs, and so on. Get a receipt and guarantee of authenticity from the seller.

Above all, buy from a reputable source. Dealers and salvage yards who sign up to the SALVO code have a sensible buying procedure for garden antiques; and other organizations such as the Art & Antiques Dealers League of America, Inc., are useful sources of information.

Restoration

The question of whether to restore or not is always a tricky one when it comes to vintage and antique gardenalia. An object has to be beautiful, but it also needs to be useful, especially if it's going to work.

As a general rule, you should never attempt to restore any garden antique of significant value. As with all antiques, poor repairs only detract from the value and you could end up doing more harm than good. There are a large number of restoration experts who specialize in statuary, metalwork, and other elements of valuable gardenalia—a quick browse on the Internet will find a suitable person near you. It many cases it may be better to do nothing at all—an item's knocks and cracks are part of its history and add to its overall appeal. There's also always a financial balance between the costs of restoration and the final value of the item. If in doubt, talk to a dealer or restoration specialist.

At the other end of the scale, most of the vintage gardenalia in this book is inexpensive—that's the great thing about it. If you want to restore it, go for it. But remember that distressed paintwork, a little bit of rust, or the odd dent can add a lot of character and you can lose something of this personality in the process of over-restoration.

The only exception to this rule is tools. Working tools, however old, need to be safe and usable. That usually means smooth surfaces to hold and all the component parts in good condition and firmly attached to each other. If you're going to use vintage tools they need to be free from cracks, woodworm, and rot, and cutting tools should be kept sharp. They will give you a lifetime of use if properly maintained.

Thefts and securities

Objects kept outside are easy pickings for thieves. Stone urns, statues, gates, and ironwork are favorite targets—the fact that they're often very heavy and need dismantling doesn't seem much of a deterrent. Even some of the more humble pieces of gardenalia get stolen—stone troughs, York paving, reclaimed bricks, chairs, and tables.

There's plenty you can do to protect your plot from gardenalia thieves. It's important to keep things in perspective—most gardenalia will happily sit untouched for years—so don't let the remote possibility of theft stop you from decorating your outside space with garden collectibles.

Four simple steps will give you peace of mind:

Think like a thief
Thieves are often opportunistic so make it as difficult as possible for someone to get in and out of

your garden undetected. High walls, hedges, fences, gates, and other physical barriers will make a quick getaway tricky and reduce the risk of casual thefts, especially from front gardens.

Keep it secure

Small items such as tools, pots, chairs, and tables can be locked away in a shed overnight if necessary, but larger valuable items may need an antitheft device. Anything very valuable should be alarmed.

Keep records

For valuable gardenalia, keep a detailed description of the item for insurance purposes. Photographs, taken from several angles if possible, and a written report will also greatly improve your chances of an item being recovered by the police.

Act quickly

If the worst should happen, contact the police immediately. Stolen garden antiques are often exported so the quicker you act the better the chance of recovery. Report the stolen item to www.artloss.com—they will search subsequent auctions to see if it reappears in the future.

RESOURCES

Adkins Architectural Antiques & Treasures
3515 Fannin Street
Houston, TX 77004
(713) 522-6547
www.adkinsantiques.com

Aileen Minor American Antiques
208 South Liberty Street
Post Office Box 410
Centreville, MD 21617
(410) 758-1489
www.aileenminor.com

Alhambra Antiques
2850 Salzedo Street
Coral Gables, FL 33134
(305) 446-1688
www.alhambraantiques.com

Amighini Architectural
www.salvageantiques.com

3429 East Coast Highway
Corona del Mar, CA 92625
(949) 673-5555

1505 N. State College Boulevard
Anaheim, CA, 92806
(714) 776-5555

246 Beacon Avenue
Jersey City, NJ 07306
(201) 222-6367

2880 Sims Road
San Diego, CA 92106
(619) 269-5963

Antique Center Mall
4434 Hollister Avenue
Santa Barbara, CA 93110
(805) 967-5700
www.antiquecentermall.com

Antique Garden Furniture Show
at The New York Botanical Garden
2900 Southern Boulevard
Bronx, NY 10458
(718) 817-8700
www.nybg.org/agf.php

Antiques & Garden Fair
at Chicago Botanic Garden
1000 Lake Cook Road
Glencoe, IL 60022
(847) 835-5440
www.chicagobotanic.org/antiques

The Antiques Garage
112 West 25th Street
New York, NY 10001
(212) 243-5343
www.hellskitchenfleamarket.com

Architectural Antiques
1330 Quincy Street NE
Minneapolis, MN 55413
(612) 332-8344
www.archantiques.com

Architectural Artifacts
20 S. Ontario
Toledo, OH 43604
(419) 243-6916
www.coolstuffiscoolstuff.com

Architectural Salvage, Inc.
3 Mill Street
Exeter, NH 03833
(603) 773-5635
www.oldhousesalvage.com

Architectural Salvage New York
246 Beacon Avenue
Jersey City, NJ 07306
(201) 222-6367
www.architecturalsalvagenewyork.com

Architectural Salvage of San Diego
2401 Kettner Boulevard
San Diego, CA 92101
(619) 696-1313
architecturalsalvagesd.com

Architectural Salvage Warehouse
11 Maple Street
Five Corners
Essex Jct, VT 05452
(802) 879-4221
www.greatsalvage.com

Architectural Salvage Warehouse of Detroit
4885 15th Street
Detroit, MI 48208
(313) 896-8333
www.aswdetroit.org

Artefact Design and Salvage
23562 Highway 121
Sonoma, CA 95476
(707) 933-0660
www.artefactdesignsalvage.com

Authentic Provence
www.authenticprovence.com

Interior Showroom
522 Clematis Street
West Palm Beach, FL 33401
(561) 805-9995

Exterior Showroom "The Secret Garden"
5600 South Dixie Highway
West Palm Beach, FL 33405
(561) 805 9995

Barbara Israel Garden Antiques
Katonah, NY 10536
(212) 744-6281
www.bi-gardenantiques.com

Brimfield Antique and Collectibles
Route 20
Brimfield, MA
(413) 283-2418
www.brimfieldshow.com

The Demolition Depot & Irreplaceable Artifacts
216 East 125th Street
New York, NY 10035
(212) 860-1138
www.demolitiondepot.com

The Elemental Garden
259 Main Street South (Route 6)
Woodbury, CT 06798
(203) 263-6500
www.theelementalgarden.com

Englishtown Auction
90 Wilson Avenue
Englishtown, NJ 07726
(732) 446-9644
www.englishtownauction.com

Fleur
10 Dakin Avenue
Mount Kisco, NY 10549
(914) 241-3400
www.fleur-newyork.com

Georgetown Flea Market
1819 35th Street NW
Washington, DC 20007
www.georgetownfleamarket.com

A Glance into the Past
410 E. Branch Street
Arroyo Grande, CA 93420
(805) 489-5666
aglanceintothepastantiques.com

Grace A Place of Restoration
918 East Broadway
Columbia, MO 65201
(573) 442-7466
www.graceplace.biz

Harwinton Antiques & Design Weekend
80 Locust Road
Harwinton, CT 06791
(317) 598-0012
www.farmingtonantiquesweekend.com

Hell's Kitchen Flea Market
West 39th Street
between 9th & 10th Avenues
New York, NY
(212) 243-5343
www.hellskitchenfleamarket.com

Historic Houseparts
540 South Avenue
Rochester, NY 14620
(585) 325-2329
www.historichouseparts.com

Inner Gardens
www.innergardens.com

6050 West Jefferson Boulevard
Los Angeles, CA 90016
(310) 838-8378

8925 Melrose Avenue
West Hollywood, CA 90069
(310) 492-9990

1324 Montana Avenue
Santa Monica, CA 90403
(310) 576-3400

Keith Merry Garden Park Antiques
7121 Cockrill Bend Boulevard
Nashville, TN 37209
(615) 350-6655
www.gardenpark.com

Kimball & Bean Architectural and Garden Antiques
3606 S. Country Club Road
Woodstock, IL 60098
(815) 444-9000
www.kimballandbean.com

Lauritzen Gardens Antique & Garden Show
100 Bancroft Street
Omaha, NE 68108
(402) 346-4002
lauritzengardens.org/Antique_Show

Le Louvre French Antiques
1400 Slocum Street
Dallas, TX 75207
(214) 742-2605
www.lelouvre-antiques.com

Legacy Vintage Building Materials & Antiques
540 Division Street
Cobourg, Ontario K9A 3S4, Canada
(905) 373-0796
www.legacyvintage.com

Long Beach Antique Market
Long Beach Veterans Stadium
4901 E Conant Street
Long Beach, CA 90808
(323) 655-5703
www.longbeachantiquemarket.com

Mecox Gardens
www.mecoxgardens.com

919 N. La Cienega Boulevard
Los Angeles, CA 90069
(310) 358-9272

3900 South Dixie Highway
West Palm Beach, FL 33405
(561) 805-8611

406 N. Clark Street
Chicago, IL 60654
(312) 836-0571

66 Newtown Lane
East Hampton, NY 11937
(631) 329-9405

962 Lexington Ave
New York, NY 10021
(212) 249-5301

257 County Road 39A
Southampton, NY 11968
(631) 287-5015

4532 Cole Avenue
Dallas, TX 75205
(214) 580-3800

3912 Westheimer Road
Houston, TX 77027
(713) 355-2100

Nor'East Architectural Antiques
16 Exeter Road
South Hampton, NH 03827
(603) 394-0006
www.noreast1.com

Ohmega Salvage
2400 San Pablo Avenue
2407 San Pablo Avenue
Berkeley, CA 94702
(510) 204-0767
www.ohmegasalvage.com

Olde Good Things
www.ogtstore.com

1800 South Grand Avenue
Los Angeles, CA 90015
(213) 746-8600

11240 West Olympic Boulevard
Los Angeles, CA 90064
(310) 477-8444

450 Columbus Avenue
New York, NY 10024
(212) 362-8025

5 East 16th Street
New York, NY 10003
(212) 989-8814

124 West 24th Street
New York, NY 10011
(212) 989-8401

400 Gilligan Street
Scranton, PA 18508
(570) 341-7668

Portland Architectural Salvage
131 Preble Street
Portland, ME 04101
(207) 780-0634
www.portlandsalvage.com

Recycling the Past
381 North Main Street
Barnegat, NJ 08005
(609) 660-9790
www.recyclingthepast.com

Rose Bowl Flea Market
1001 Rose Bowl Drive
Pasadena, CA 91103
(323) 560-7469
www.rgcshows.com

Rose Garden Antiques and Design
Rock City Road 2
Red Hook, NY 12457
(646) 249-7480
www.rosegardenantiques.com

Sarasota Architectural Salvage
1093 Central Avenue
Sarasota, FL 34236
(941) 362-0803
www.sarasotasalvage.com

Scavenger's Paradise
5453 Satsuma Avenue
North Hollywood, CA 91601
(323) 877-7945
www.scavengersparadise.com

Scott Antiques Markets
(740) 569-2800
www.scottantiquemarket.com

3650 Jonesboro Road Southeast
Atlanta, GA 30354

717 East 17th Avenue
Columbus, OH 43211

Silver Fox Salvage
www.silverfoxsalvage.com

20 Learned Street
Albany, NY 12207
(518) 256-3955

1060 E. Cesar E. Chavez
Los Angeles, CA 90033
(323) 225-5385

Silverado Salvage and Design
(760) 453-6293
www.silveradosalvageanddesign.com

The Thompson Studio
Berwyn, Chester County, PA
(610) 644-1110
www.thethompsonstudio.com

Three Potato Four
376 Shurs Lane
Building A
Philadelphia, PA 19128
(267) 335-3633
www.threepotatofourshop.com

Three Speckled Hens Antiques and Old Stuff
P.O. Box 850
Templeton, CA 93465
(805) 674-7807
www.threespeckledhens.com

Tivoli Garden Antiques
107 E. Main Street
Barrington, IL 60010
(847) 756-4174
www.tivoligardenantiques.com

Trellis & Trugs
3372B Commercial Avenue
Northbrook, IL 60062
(847) 784-6910
trellisandtrugs.com

The Vintage Garden
201 W. College Avenue
Appleton, WI 54911
(920) 407-1366
thevintagegarden.org

West 25th Street Market
West 25th Street
between Broadway and 6th Avenue
New York, NY
(212) 243-5343
www.hellskitchenfleamarket.com

William Laman
Furniture. Garden. Antiques
1496 East Valley Road
Montecito, CA 93108
(805) 969-2840
www.williamlaman.com

Yard Art
UniqueGardenDecor.com
411 Hartz Avenue
Suite R
Danville, CA 94526
(925) 234-3153

INDEX

PICTURE CREDITS

1 Country Living/ Hester Page; 2 Philippe Perdereau/ Les Jardins de Roquelin; 4 Istockphotos.com; 4–5 Country Living/ Jason Ingram; 5 Istockphotos.com; 6–7 www.marycarrollphotography.com; 8 Nicola Stocken Tomkins/ The Garden Collection; 9 left Laura Moss; 9 right Laura Moss; 10 left Laura Moss; 10 right Laura Moss; 11 Laura Moss;12/13 Philippe Perdereau/ Design: C. Yverneau, France; 14 © Andrea Jones/ Garden Exposures Picture Library/ Design: Owner, Lucy MacKenzie Pannizzon, Lip na Cloiche, Isle of Mull, Scotland; 15 Philippe Perdereau/ Jardin Poterie Hillen, France; 16 Mark Bolton, Garden Picture Library, Photolibrary U.K.; 17 Philippe Perdereau/ Jardin Poterie Hillen, France; 18 Philippe Perdereau/ Design: Alexandre Thomas, France; 19 Mayer le Scanff/ Les jardins de Maizicourt 80 France; 20 above Mayer le Scanff/ Le Jardin de Berchigranges 88 France; 20 below Mayer le Scanff/ Le Jardin de Berchigranges 88 France; 21 MMGI / Marianne Majerus/ Design: Ruth Collier; 22 Simon Upton / The Interior Archive/ John Fowler designed the garden, Nicholas Haslam is the current tenant; 23 above left Marion Brenner/ Designer: Lisa Moseley; 23 above right Country Living/ Jason Ingram; 23 below left Clive Nichols/ Wollerton Hall, Shropshire; 23 below right Philippe Perdereau/ Design: Sonja Gauron, France; 24 Mark Bolton, Garden Picture Library, Photolibrary U.K.; 25 Country Living/ Emma Lee; 26 Philippe Perdereau/ Design: Dina Deferme, Belgium; 27 left Helen Fickling/ The Interior Archive; 27 right Country Living; 28 Andreas von Einsiedel; 29 Mark Turner, Garden Picture Library, Photolibrary U.K.; 30 Johner Images/ Getty; 31 above left Country Living/ Robin Matthews; 31 below left © Andrea Jones/Garden Exposures Photo Library/ Design: Chris O'Donoghue; 31 right Garden Picture Library, Photolibrary U.K.; 32 above Country Living/ Andrea Jones; 32 below GAP Photos/Anne Green-Armytage; 33 Jane Sebire/ Glebe Garden; 34 Philippe Perdereau; 35 Andreas von Einsiedel; 36 left Philippe Perdereau/ Oak Tree Cottage 36 center Bonnie Manion, author/photographer, www.VintageGardenGal.com.; 36 right Philippe Perdereau/ Bryan's Ground Garden; 37 Marion Brenner/ The Gardener, Healdsburg CA; 38 above left © Andrea Jones/Garden Exposures Photo Library/ Design: Owners, Marcus and Anne Binney, Domaine des Vaux, St Lawrence, Jersey; 38 above right Philippe Perdereau/ Design: C. Yverneau, France; 38 below © Andrea Jones/Garden Exposures Photo Library/ Design: Owners, Rick Darke and Melinda Zoehrer, Landenberg, PA, USA; 40 left Clive Nichols/ The Walled Garden at Cowdray, West Sussex/ Designer: Jan Howard; 40 right © Andrea Jones/Garden Exposures Photo Library/ Design: del Buono Gazerwitz Landscape Architecture; 41 Marion Brenner/ Nancy Heckler Designer; 42 Andreas von Einsiedel; 43 Philippe Perdereau/ Coach House Garden; 44 © Andrea Jones/Garden Exposures Photo Library/ Design: Owners, Gail and Raymond Paul, Braid Farm, Road, Edinburgh, Scotland; 45 Richard Felber, Garden Picture Library, Photolibrary U.K.; 46 Philippe Perdereau/ Sculpture by Michel Perrier, France; 47 Philippe Perdereau/ Mawley Garden; 48-49 © Andrea Jones/ Garden Exposures Picture Library/ Design: Owner, Lucy MacKenzie Pannizzon, Lip na Cloiche, Isle of Mull, Scotland; 50 above Country Living/ Jason Ingram; 50 below Philippe Perdereau/ La Mansoniere, France; 51 MMGI/ Bennet Smith/ Wildwood, Kent; 52 left © Andrea Jones/ Garden Exposures Photo Library/ Design: Northwind Perennial Farm, WI, USA; 52 right © Red Cover/Photoshot; 53 MMGI/ Marianne Majerus/ Clinton Lodge, Sussex; 54 above left Mayer le Scanff/ Lanscapers: Soucat & Bourry, Domaine de Chaumont-sur-Loire 41 France; 54 above right Philippe Perdereau/ Les Jardins de Maizicourt, France; 54 below left Andreas von Einsiedel; 54 below right Philippe Perdereau/ Design: Maurieres & Ossart, Jardin des Paradis, France; 55 Philippe Perdereau/ Rose Garden Francia Thauvin, France; 56 left Juliette Wade, Garden Picture Library, Photolibrary U.K.; 56 right © Andrea Jones/Garden Exposures Photo Library/ Design: Owner, Ros Bissell, Moors Meadow Garden and Nursery, Bromyard, Herefordshire; 57 Philippe Perdereau/ Jardin Enteoulet, France; 58 Country Living; 59 Philippe Perdereau/ Jardin en Seine, France; 60 Andreas von Einsiedel; 61 Narratives / A. Mezza & E. Escalante; 62 above left Nicolas Matheus/ Cote Sud/ Designer: Josephine Ryan; 62 above right Ron Evans/ Garden Picture Library/ Getty; 62 below left Country Living/ Alex Ramsay; 62 below right Philippe Perdereau 63 Country Living; 64 left Philippe Perdereau/ Design: C. Yverneau, France; 64 right Country Living; 65 Country Living/ Charlie Colmer; 66–67 Simon Upton/ The Interior Archive/ Designer: J. Morgan Puett; 68 © Andrea Jones/Garden Exposures Photo Library/ Design: Owners, Gail and Raymond

Paul Braid Farm, Road, Edinburgh, Scotland; 69 © IPC+Syndication; 70 left Country Living/ Richard Bloom; 70 right Alan Wilkes; 71 Andreas von Einsiedel; 72 Simon Wheeler, Garden Picture Library, Photolibrary U.K.; 73 above Country Living/ Charlie Colmer; 73 below Nicola Stocken Tomkins/The Garden Collection; 74 above left Garden World Images/C. Niele; 74 above right MMGI/ Marianne Majerus/ Design: Marianne Jacoby; 74 below MMGI/Marianne Majerus/ Lowder Mill, Sussex; 75 MMGI/ Marianne Majerus; 76 Philippe Perdereau/ Design: Helly van Baalen, Netherlands; 77 MMGI/ Marianne Majerus/ Design: Claire Mee; 78 GAP Photos/ Zara Napier - Design: Isobel Bilgen 79 above left Country Living/ Cristian Barnett; 79 above right Chris Tubbs; 79 below left GAP Photos/ Michael King; 79 below right Country Living/ Cristian Barnett; 80 left Country Living/ Jason Ingram; 80 right Eric van Lokven/The Garden Collection; 81 Country Living; 82 MMGI/ Marianne Majerus/ Design: Claire Mee; 83 above left Mark Bolton, Garden Picture Library, Photolibrary U.K.; 83 above right Mark Bolton, Garden Picture Library, Photolibrary U.K.; 83 center right Andre Baranowski, Images.com, Photolibrary U.K.; 83 below left Country Living/ Alun Callender; 83 below right Garden Picture Library, Photolibrary U.K.; 84 Country Living; 85 Mayer le Scanff; 86 © DreyerHensley@taverne-agency.com; 88 Jane Sebire/ Mount St John Walled Vegetable Garden; 89 Country Living/ Nicola Stocken Tomkins; 90 Juliette Wade, Garden Picture Library, Photolibrary U.K.; 91 Philippe Perdereau/ Les Jardins de Roquelin; 92 above Cora Niele, Garden Picture Library, Photolibrary U.K.; 92 below © Andrea Jones/Garden Exposures Photo Library/ Design: RHS Harlow Carr, Harrogate, Yorkshire; 93 Garden World Images/ L. Heusinkveld; 94 Jo Campbell; 95 above left © Andrea Jones/ Garden Exposures Photo Library; 95 above right Country Living/ Kate Gadsby; 95 below left © Andrea Jones/ Garden Exposures Picture Library/ Design: Owner, Lucy MacKenzie Pannizzon, Lip na Cloiche, Isle of Mull, Scotland; 95 below right © Andrea Jones/ Garden Exposures Picture Library/ Design: Owner, Lucy MacKenzie Pannizzon, Lip na Cloiche, Isle of Mull, Scotland; 96 above Country Living; 96 below Philippe Perdereau; 97 Country Living/ James Merrell; 98 Istockphotos.com; 98-100 All pictures: Jo Campbell; 103 Istockphotos.com; 102–105 All pictures: Mayer le Scanff/ Les Jardins du Prieuré Notre Dame d'Orsan 18 France; 106 Philippe Perdereau/ Design: Dina Deferme, Belgium 107 Country Living/ Brent Darby; 108 © IPC+Syndication; 109 above Country Living/ Simon Bevan; 109 below Laura Moss/ Taylor Interior Design, Styling by Stacy Kunstel; 110 Philippe Perdereau/ Maisons Marines, France; 111 Ryan Benyi Photography; 112 Narratives / Jan Baldwin; 113 top left Alan Wilkes, 113 above right MMGI/ Marianne Majerus/ Design: Marty Hoffmann; 113 below left © Andrea Jones/Garden Exposures Photo Library/ Design: Northwind Perennial Farm, WI, USA; 113 below right Marion Brenner/ Thomas Hobbes, Vancouver BC Canada; 114 Istockphotos.com; 114–117 All pictures: Andreas von Einsiedel; 118 Istockphotos.com; 118–21 All pictures: Anna Kern/ House of Pictures/ Styling: Inger Wachtmester/ House of Pictures; 122 Philippe Perdereau/ Design: Walda Pairon, Belgium; 123 Alan Wilkes; 124–25 MMGI/ Marianne Majerus/ Wollerton Old Hall, Shropshire; 126 Clive Nichols/ Wollerton Hall, Shropshire; 127 Alan Wilkes; 129 Istockphotos.com; 128–131 Clive Nichols/ Designer: Dominique Lafourcade, Provence, France; 132 Istockphotos.com; 132–35 Clive Nichols/ The Walled Garden at Cowdray, West Sussex/ Designer: Jan Howard; 136 Marion Brenner/ Shirley Watts Design, Alameda CA; 137 Garden Picture Library, Photolibrary U.K.; 138 Philippe Perdereau; 139 left © Andrea Jones/Garden Exposures Photo Library/ Design: Owners, The Howard Family, Colonsay House, Isle of Colonsay, Scotland; 139 right Country Living/ Charlie Colmer; 140 Simon Upton/ The Interior Archive/ Designer: Arne Maynard; 141 Simon Upton/ The Interior Archive/ Designer: J. Morgan Puett; 142–43 MMGI/ Marianne Majerus/ Trevoole Farm, Cornwall; 144 MMGI/ Marianne Majerus/ Trevoole Farm, Cornwall; 145 Marion Brenner/ Botanica/ Getty; 146 Marion Brenner/ Sabrina Judge Design, Los Angeles; 147 above left Andreas von Einsiedel; 147 above center Country Living/ Caroline Arber; 147 above right Sean Maylon. Garden Picture Library, Photolibrary U.K.; 147 below left Gary Rogers/ The Garden Collection; 147 below right Philippe Perdereau/ Design: Michel Semini, France; 148 Istockphotos.com; 148-151 All pictures: www.marycarrollphotography.com; 153 Istockphotos.com; 152–155 all pictures: Jennifer Cheung/ Botanica/ Getty; 156 Philippe Perdereau/ Jardin Silene, Belgium; 157 Marcus Harpur/

Design: Francine Raymond, Suffolk; 158 David C Phillips, Garden Photo World, Photolibrary U.K.; 159 Philippe Perdereau/ Imig Garden, Germany; 160-161 Philippe Perdereau; 162 Philippe Perdereau/ Design: Nina Balthau, Belgium; 163 above Andreas von Einsiedel; 163 below MMGI/ Marianne Majerus/ Trevoole Farm, Cornwall; 164 Istockphotos.com; 164–67 All pictures: Jonathan Buckley/ Designer: Sarah Raven, Perch Hill www.sarahraven.com; 168 Philippe Giraud, Bios, Photolibrary U.K.; 169 Clive Nichols/ Rose Gray and David Macilwaine; 170 left Country Living/ Emma Lee; 170 right Philippe Perdereau/ Bender Lucenz Garden, Germany; 171 left MMGI/ Marianne Majerus/ Design: Jamie Dunstan; 171 right Philippe Perdereau/ Jardin Silene, Belgium; 172 above Country Living/ Alun Callender; 172 below Philippe Perdereau/ Jardins des Salines, France; 173 MMGI/ Marianne Majerus/ Design: Nada Habet; 174 Garden Pix Ltd, Photolibrary U.K.; 175 Garden Pix, Photolibrary U.K.; 176 GAP Photos/Mark Bolton – Design Penny Smith; 177 Claire Takacs, Photolibrary U.K.; 178 Garden Pix, Photolibrary U.K.; 180 above Moodboard, Photolibrary U.K.; 180 below Country Living/ Michelle Garrett; 181 © IPC+Syndication; 183 Istockphotos.com; 184 Istockphotos.com; 182–87 All pictures: Victoria Harley/ Styling: Sally Coulthard and Victoria Harley; 188 Photoshot, Red Cover, Photolibrary U.K.; 189 Country Living/ Charlie Colmer; 190 Philippe Perdereau/ Jardin Pomme d'Ambre, France; 191 left Country Living/ Kate Gadsby; 191 right Country Living/ Simon Bevan; 192 Country Living/ Huntley Hedworth; 193 Country Living/ Emma Lee; 194 Istockphotos.com; 194–97 All pictures: Victoria Harley/ Styling: Sally Coulthard, Victoria Harley and Laura Woussen; 198 Istockphotos.com; 198–201 All pictures: Steven Randazzo Photography; 202 MMGI / Marianne Majerus/ Design: Aileen Scoula; 203 © Andrea Jones/Garden Exposures Photo Library/ Design: Adrian Hallam, Chris Arrowsmith and Nigel Dunnet; 204 Marion Brenner/ James Doyle Design Associates; 205 above left Philippe Perdereau/ Jardin Chateau de Rivau, France; 205 above right © Andrea Jones/ Garden Exposures Photo Library/ Design: Lord and Lady Russell, Park House, Woburn Estate, Bedfordshire; 205 below left Country Living/ Pia Tryde; 205 below right Clive Nichols/ Designer: Bunny Guinness/ DGAA Homelife Garden, Chelsea 97; 206 Sebastian Siraudeau / Cote Ouest; 207 GAP Photos/FhF Greenmedia; 209 Istockphotos.com; 208–11 Tiffany Kirchner Dixon; 212 Philippe Perdereau/ Garden Bijsterveld; 215 Country Living/ Pia Tryde; Front endpapers Philippe Perdereau/ Jardin Silene, Belgium; Back endpapers Jerry Harpur/ Design: Cary Wolinsky, Mass, U.S.A.

On the jacket: author photograph Andrea Denniss; front Philippe Perdereau/ Design: C. Yverneau, France; Back: above left Laura Moss/ Taylor Interior Design, styling by Stacy Kunstel; above right MMGI/ Marianne Majerus/ Clinton Lodge, Sussex; below left Alan Wilkes; below right: Marcus Harpur/ Design: Francine Raymond, Suffolk

Acknowledgments

Many thanks to everyone who brought *Gardenalia* to fruition, especially Jacqui Small, Jo Copestick, Kerenza Swift, Sian Parkhouse, Claire Hamilton, and Peter Colley. It's a joy working with such lovely, creative people. Thanks also to Laura Woussen, who's done an excellent job making the book look so beautiful; Victoria Harley for her delightful photographs; and Liz Somers for her PR expertise.

Thanks to my wonderful family—I promise this is a real job.

This book is dedicated to little Isabella.